5/14

The Day the Devil Came to Buffalo

Foreword by Jacquie Abram

International Best-Selling & Award-Winning Author of
Hush Money: How One Woman Proved Systemic Racism in
her Workplace & Kept her Job

MARK TALLEY

Table of Contents

Foreword by Jacquie Abram

My name is Jacquie Abram and I'm the international best-selling and award-winning author of *Hush Money: How One Woman Proved Systemic Racism in her Workplace and Kept her Job.* Hush Money is a book that I wrote from a place of pain after my lucrative career in higher education was killed by racists and I found myself homeless and contemplating homicide and suicide.

On May 14, 2022, I was writing my third book and listening to MSNBC in the background, when I heard a breaking news story that caught my attention. I quickly turned the volume on the TV up as the news anchor reported that a racially motivated mass shooting had occurred in Buffalo leaving ten dead and three injured. When I heard this news, my heart fell into my stomach because the majority of my relatives on my mother's side reside in Buffalo and Niagara Falls.

Immediately, I started reaching out to family members on Facebook trying to verify that everyone was accounted for. But when one of my aunts had gone shopping and couldn't be found, the fear I felt for her was overwhelming. It was the type of fear that you wouldn't wish on your worst enemy.

Fortunately, my aunt was located shopping at a store in west Buffalo an hour later and words cannot begin to describe how relieved I was for her and our family. But my heart hurt for the people in east Buffalo who weren't so lucky, and I wanted to see about them because although I couldn't take away the pain they experienced from racism in their community, I did have something of value to help them fight back against racism in their workplaces, a place many of them still had to return to even after experiencing such a horrific tragedy. So, an event was planned in October 2022 and arrangements were made for me to come to Buffalo to give away hundreds of free Hush Money books that had been sponsored by loving allies of the Black community.

On July 11, 2022, Mark Talley sent me a message on Linkedin. "I hear you're coming to Buffalo," he said.

When I confirmed that I was coming to Buffalo, he asked if he could help me with my event. And when I asked him what he wanted to do to help, the next thing he said had me frozen in my seat. "I don't know if you know who I am, but my mom was shopping for groceries at Tops and was killed by a racist."

After reading his message, I requested to speak with him, and we immediately jumped on a call. And when I asked him how he knew who I was, he said, "I read both of your Hush Money books and I was moved by them because everything you said you experienced from racism at work is what I'm experiencing now."

5/14: The Day the Devil Came to Buffalo is a powerful story that takes you on a journey into Mark's life before, during, and after the racially-motivated terrorist attack at Tops Friendly Market that took his mother away from him. You will laugh, you will cry, and your heart will hurt. But I promise you, when you come out of his journey, you will be inspired to do something more than offering thoughts and prayers the next time you hear a breaking news story about another mass shooting.

I've met a lot of people since writing Hush Money, but I have to say that none have had a greater impact on me than Mark Talley. And although the ways that racists targeted us were different, the end result was the same—racial trauma and it was that racial trauma that brought us together.

I am deeply humbled and honored to have been selected by Mark to not only write the Foreword to this powerful book, but also to collaborate with him on telling his story and publishing his book. I will always be grateful to Mark for seeking me out after he read *Hush Money: How One Woman Proved Systemic Racism in her Workplace & Kept her Job* and the sequel *Hush Money: The Cost of Being Black in Corporate America* and for the value he found in me and my experiences with racism in the workplace that broke me and nearly destroyed me.

Preface
Hey Mama – Kanye West

My name is Mark Talley and I'm thirty-three years old. Despite going to a Catholic high school and having somewhat of a Baptist upbringing, I've never been an overly religious kind of guy—never gave much thought to the concepts of good and evil.

But something happened.

Something that shook me to my core.

Something that convinced me that the devil is real.

The date was May 14, 2022, a day that will go down in history as the day the devil, disguised as a racist asshole with hate in his heart and a semiautomatic rifle, came to the eastside of Buffalo and killed ten innocent Black people at Tops Friendly Market. Geraldine C. Talley, my sixty-two-year-old mother, was one of them. She was the last person he killed with two shots to the head before police "calmly" arrested him. I guess I can find a little solace in the fact that they didn't take him to

Burger King afterwards like they did when Dylann Roof, that other racist asshole, murdered nine Black people during Bible study and worship at their church.[1]

Even though a year has passed since my mom was killed, there are days when I still can't mentally wrap my head around the fact that she's gone. I find myself some days just staring aimlessly at her driver's license, credit cards, and social security cards tearing up and hoping she'll call me. I still have her listed on my phone as my medical emergency contact in case something happens to me. When I have family problems with her siblings or my sister, I send her a playful but emotional message hoping she'll respond and take care of everything…. Unfortunately, I have yet to get a response, a response I desperately need.

Then there are other days. Days when my heart hurts so much because I know I'm never going to see her again. Days when I spend hours reading and rereading old messages that we sent to each other. Days when I wish I could pay her cell phone bill hoping she will pick up if I call her so I can hear her country accent just one more time. And days when I'm so angry at her for going to Tops instead of a bodega, a Family Dollar, a Dollar General, or whatever to get some deli meat.

Sometimes, when I'm lying awake in bed, minutes after waking up, missing my mother, and feeling an emptiness inside, I find myself thinking about the song Kanye West (The Old Kanye) performed in Paris one week after his mother died. In the song, *Hey Mama,* Kanye sang, *"Last night I saw you in my dreams, now I can't wait to go to sleep."*[2]

Ever since the day my mother died, sleeping has been one of the best parts of my reality because when I sleep, I dream. When I dream, she's not dead—she's alive. So, for me, sleep represents little slices of life because it's the portal to my dreams, a place where my mom still exists, and I'm free to feel all the emotions hidden deep inside me. I rarely feel those emotions when I'm awake, not only due to my introverted nature, but also because I show behaviors that are characteristic of Asperger's Syndrome, I am told. This combination makes it almost impossible for the emotions I feel on the inside to match the emotions—or lack thereof—displayed on the outside. And when you add in the dark humor that I now realize I've been using to cope with my mom's unexpected death, some people think that I just don't care about her or have a lack of empathy. On social media, I've had people message me saying "You're glad your mother is dead" or comment on posts I make saying "I don't think he even loved his mother". Someone even made a comment saying that "He's trying to profit off the death of his mother" after I announced that I was writing a book.

I've spent many hours over the last year retracing my steps on May 14th from the time I awoke to the time my mother was killed and wondering if there was something I could've done to change her fate. You know—maybe there was some cosmic sign I should've seen or some divine message I may have missed.

But there is one thing I know for sure. If I had known on the morning of May 14th, 2022, that by 2:28 p.m. my mother would be dead, I would've done so many things differently that day. I would've stopped by her house and told her how much I love her. I would've thanked her for raising me as a single parent. I would've hugged her tight and apologized for being such a bull-headed kid growing up. And most importantly, I would've slashed the tires on her car to keep her home that day or waited for her killer at the store and used my Rambo knife—as I call it—to slice and dice his face so bad, no one would question the reason for a closed casket at his funeral.

But the Universe had other plans that day.

---

1.   Kinnard, Meg and Lavoie, Denise. "Court upholds death sentence for church shooter Dylann Roof." AP News, August 25, 2021. https://apnews.com/article/religion-389bcc56019f268cb1056e37a517bd6c

2.   West, Kanye. "Hey Mama (Grammy Remix) Lyrics." Lyrics on Demand, (n.d.). https://www.lyricsondemand.com/k/kanyewestlyrics/heymamagrammyremixlyrics.html

Chapter 1
Dear Mama – Tupac Shakur

⚖

During my early childhood years living in Buffalo, New York, I felt like I had it all. I had a father who worked hard to provide for our family; a sister I enjoyed being around; a mother that I adored; and most importantly, plenty of time to spend with my grandparents. At five years old, I enjoyed being with my grandparents the most whether I was with both of them junking on weekends in search of aluminum, with my grandfather drinking tiny sips of wine, or with my grandmother who was an amazing cook.

Luckily, my grandmother passed her cooking skills along to my mother who had the cooking skills of a five-star chef. To me, this was her most important quality because she loved to cook as much as I loved to eat.

The bond between me and my mom grew in 1998 after we moved to a small suburb in Florida about twenty miles from Orlando. Why we moved—no idea. This was one of the few times that I stayed in a child's place and didn't bother to ask any questions. I was nine years old at the time and because my sister no longer lived with us, I found myself spending more time with my mother after she picked me up from school. That's when I discovered that there was more to her than just cooking delicious meals and baking delectable desserts. What I discovered was something we would consistently fight about over the next two decades.

Me with my mom at age 7

I'll never forget the day I realized that she was big into horoscopes. She was sitting at the kitchen table drinking a cup of lemon water and flipping pages in the newspaper.

"There's my double scoop of dark chocolate," she said as I walked up and sat down at the table with her.

I smiled. "What are you doing?"

"Reading my horoscope. I read it every day."

"What the heck are horoscopes?" I asked. "Does dad read his horoscope?"

"No, baby," she chuckled. "Your dad doesn't read his horoscope."

"You can read me my horoscope if you want."

My mom's eyes lit up like sparklers on the Fourth of July. "Well, Mark," she excitedly said. "The first thing you need to know is that your personality is part Cancer and part Gemini."

Then, she proceeded to read my horoscope for that day, and I actively listened to every word she read.

When she finished, she looked up from her newspaper and saw me grinning like a Cheshire cat. "What do you think of your horoscope?" she asked before taking a sip of lemon water.

"Well mom, I think you're too old to be reading this magical nonsense."

Suddenly, my mom burst into laughter and started spitting lemon water all over me and my horoscope!

Things in Florida were good for a while, but shortly after I turned ten years old, things started to change. That's when I began noticing things about my mom that my younger self never noticed.

Strange things.

Peculiar things.

One thing that I noticed was that my mom wasn't like the other mom's her age. She was an old soul, a very old soul, and because of the way she acted, the kind of things she enjoyed, and her personality in general, I began to think she was a sixty-year-old woman trapped in a forty-year-old body. I mean—it was strange that someone her age enjoyed watching old black and white movies when there were so many other movies she could watch in color. And I thought it was really peculiar that she bought a printed newspaper every day to get her daily dose of news instead of watching it on TV.

One day, I was playing video games in my bedroom after school. Two hours later, I got hungry and went to find my mom. I looked in her bedroom—she wasn't there. I walked down the hallway thinking she was in the kitchen, but when I turned the corner, there she was. Sitting on the couch in the living room watching an old black and white movie and thumbing through the newspaper *at the same time*!

I stood in the hallway rapidly blinking my eyes, and staring at her like she was some kind of mutant.

"Hey baby," she said, looking up from her newspaper. "You gettin' hungry?"

"Yes, can you order pizza?"

"Your dad will be here in about fifteen minutes. I'll order a pizza then."

I glanced at the clock on the wall. It was 5:45 p.m. *I'll be glad when six o'clock gets here,* I thought to myself.

I started to walk away, then I stopped and turned around to give my mom some helpful advice. "Did you know you can get all the news you want right on your TV? The morning news, the nightly news, and the middle of the day news, too."

My mom smiled. "Yes, I know."

"And, you may not have noticed, but movies are made in color now."

"Mark, hush up," she chuckled, rolling her eyes at me.

I gave my mom a kiss on the cheek, went back to my bedroom, and resumed playing video games.

I was so immersed in my game that I forgot about being hungry and lost track of time—that is, until my stomach growled louder than a grizzly bear. I looked at the clock on my nightstand. "Seven-thirty!" I said out loud.

I rushed back to the living room. "Moooom! I'm starving! Where's dad? Where's the pizza?"

"Not now Mark," she said, feverishly typing on her cell phone.

"But mom—"

"Mark, go make yourself a sandwich. I'll be back—"

"I can't make a sandwich. We're out of mayonnaise."

"Eat some cereal, then."

"Cereal is for breakfast, mom, I need dinner food."

Everything I said went in one of my mom's ears and out the other as she put on her sweater and grabbed her purse and keys from the kitchen table.

"Mark, I'll be back," she said, sounding panicked. "I'm locking the door. Do *not* open it for anyone, you hear me?"

"Yes, I hear you."

After my mom left, I made myself a peanut butter and jelly sandwich, grabbed a soda, and sat in the living room. As I flipped through the channels trying to find something to watch, I felt nervous on the inside, but on the outside—nothing.

Three hours later, I heard someone unlocking the door. Then, my mom walked in with a blank look on her face. "Where's dad?" I asked as she took off her sweater. "Are you ordering pizza now?"

She didn't say a word. She just dropped her keys and purse on the kitchen table, fell into the chair, and buried her face into both hands as she cried.

I was sitting on the couch in the living room in an internal state of shock because I'd never seen my mom cry before. And although I knew she wasn't a low emotions person like me—I always assumed that the reason she never cried was because she was either happy all the time or was some kind of super woman made of Teflon.

Seeing my mom cry that day helped me see her humanity and made me realize that she wasn't a super woman, she was a regular woman with feelings and emotions. A regular woman who needed me as much as I needed her.

Although I was a low emotions kid, I walked over and did my best to comfort her. "I figured it out for myself, mom," I said, hugging her with my little kid arms as she continued to cry. "Dad's not coming back. But what I don't know is why."

My mom slowly lifted her face from her tear-soaked hands and looked at me through swollen eyes. "You're too young to understand."

"Mom, I'm not just your double scoop of dark chocolate. I'm the man of the house now and I need to know what's going on."

My mom paused for a minute. Then she explained that my dad had secretly become addicted to drugs and abandoned us.

"It's okay. You don't need to cry. You got this. You're stronger than this," I insisted. "You need to man up. You control your emotions, they don't control you, that's what you always say. Plus, you still got me, and we can be strong together."

"You're right," she replied, choking back her tears. "But baby, I can't afford this place and you're too young to work."

"Then, let's go back to Buffalo. Let's move on."

"Okay," she said, kissing me on the forehead. "We'll go back home."

My mom became a single parent that day. But for me, she became both mom and dad. And I didn't mind leaving Florida because I was growing weary of the heat and flies, so I had my bags packed and was ready to go. And honestly, it really didn't matter where we lived, as long as we were together, I had everything I needed.

After selling most of our belongings, we moved back to Buffalo where my mom had several siblings and several nieces and nephews. And with a little financial help from one of my uncles, she rented a house for us, enrolled me in middle school, and things were great, for the most part.

During the next two years, I had a major growth spurt and by age twelve, I was standing six-foot-two. And because I was taller than my aunts, uncles, and cousins; towered over my mom who was only five-foot-six; and had even developed facial hair, I upgraded my title from man of the house to king of the castle and decided right then and there that nobody was going to tell me nothing.

In September 2001, I decided to put my newfound status to the test. The middle school I attended was closed for a Teacher In-service and I didn't have school that day. So, my mom woke me up at 7 a.m. "Mark, I need you to roll the garbage can to the curb before two-thirty," she said. "It's overflowing and I don't want to miss our weekly pickup. Understand?"

Me standing with my mom at age 12

"Yeah, mom," I replied, sleepily.

"Mark, this is important. Repeat what I said."

"You want me to roll the trash can to the curb by two-thirty. I got it."

My mom blew me a kiss from the doorway. "Thank you, honey. Love you!"

After my mom left, I decided to sleep in and immediately fell back to sleep.

At 11:15 a.m., I woke up and put on a loose pair of basketball shorts with a muscle shirt. And after eating three bowls of cereal, I started playing video games.

At 12:30 p.m., the house phone rang. "Hey baby," my mom said. "I'm on my lunch break. Did you take the trash to the curb?"

"Not yet, but I'm getting ready to right now."

"Okay, great. Love you, honey!"

I hung up the phone. *I'm the king of this castle,* I thought to myself as I resumed playing my video game. *I'll take it when I'm ready.*

I must admit, I loved having the house to myself as much as I loved not going to school. I felt free. I felt grown up. I could eat what I wanted; sleep when I wanted; and do what I wanted, and there was no one there to complain. I had the greatest day and felt like the king of the world, not just the king of the castle.

At about 4:30 p.m., I heard the garage door opening followed by the sound of mom's car pulling in. "Mark!" my mom screamed as she opened the inner door and walked into the living room. "Come here!"

I confidently walked down the hall. "I know you're mad about the trash," I said. "I decided to do it next week."

"I told you to take it out today and—"

"I'm the king of this castle, mom. I decide when I'll take it out."

Now, my mom was born and raised in the Deep South and had never gone sailing or even set one foot on a ship, but the language she used as she screamed and yelled at me could put a sailor to shame. I honestly couldn't believe the colorful language she was using and why she refused to listen to me. So, I did what any self-respecting king of the castle would do in my position. I put my arms around her waist and picked her up off the ground.

The next thing that I knew, my mom was wiggling, cursing, and flailing her arms like a crazy person. She wiggled so much that I had no choice but to let her go. Immediately afterwards, she marched to her bedroom, grabbed her leather belt, and came back swinging it, trying to whoop me. I thought it was funny, so I started ducking and dodging and every time she missed, I laughed.

Suddenly, she swung that belt just right and when the leather connected to my bare leg, I experienced a hot, stinging pain that was the worst I ever felt. "Owww!" I cried, falling to the ground, and writhing in pain. "You hit me! How could you?"

"Oh, we're just getting started, smart ass!" She lifted the belt to hit me again.

"Mom, stop!" I pleaded, holding my hand up in defense as tears rolled down my cheeks. "I'm your double scoop of dark chocolate!"

"Double scoop of dark chocolate my ass!" she screamed. "You better not ever call yourself disrespecting me again! I brought you into this world and I can take you out! You hear me, Mark!"

"Yes! I hear you! I hear you!"

"Now, go to your room and no video games for a month!"

I stood up and slowly made the walk of shame to my room. "I can't even be the man of the house," I muttered as my pride disappeared before my eyes, along with my status as the king of the castle.

I lost my ego that day but gained a ton of respect for my mom. I'd never seen that side of her, and although it was scary, it did my heart good to know that she wasn't the type of woman to put up with B.S. from me or anyone else. I also think my father knew about my mom's other side and maybe that's why he chose to end their marriage the cowardly way instead of just being a man and telling her to her face that he wanted out. But I honestly didn't care what his reasons were for ending their marriage the way he did. He may not have needed my mom anymore, but I firmly believed that she was the only female I'd ever need. If only I had known that another female would come along and cause me to question my beliefs.

Chapter 2
Mama Said – Lukas Graham

Moving back to buffalo after my dad abandoned us was the best decision for my mom because she was an extremely extroverted individual who valued family above all else. And with most of her siblings living in Buffalo, there wasn't time for her to be depressed between working a full-time job, taking care of me, and spending every ounce of free time she had with her sisters, brothers, nieces, and nephews.

My mom considered herself to be a Baptist Christian, even though she never went to church, and was definitely a woman of faith. And since one of my uncles had become a pastor while we were living in Florida and had started his own church, my mom told him that we would attend for at least three weeks to show our support.

At the end of church service on the third week, my uncle and other members of our family came to our house. And while the women went to the kitchen and helped my mom cook food, the men stayed in the living room. "So, Mark," my uncle said, grinning from ear to ear. "What do you think of our church service?"

"Well, I think your church service is part B.S. and part magical nonsense."

"Whaaat?" my uncle exclaimed, looking at me like I had just farted.

"Hush up, Mark!" my mom yelled from the kitchen.

Although it did my heart good to see my mom enjoying herself while spending time with our relatives, I started feeling like the black sheep of our family and really didn't like being around them. It wasn't because I didn't love them…. I think, but mainly because of two things: an age gap that made it impossible for me to get close to any of them and the fact that I'm not that much of a family person.

The age gap for family members who were younger than me was at least four to seven years, and teenage me wasn't trying to get close to them. The age gap for family members who were older than me was big, but because they were old souls like my mom with a mental age gap that was much bigger, I couldn't relate to them and vice versa.

My mom knew I wasn't close to anyone in my family besides her and although she tried to help me see the value in close family ties, she didn't hold it against me, in fact sometimes she would help me remain incognito.

I'll never forget the day we were talking in the kitchen as she stirred the ingredients for a cheesecake she was making from scratch.

Suddenly, the house phone rang, and she immediately answered it on speaker. "Hello?"

"Hey Auntie Gerri, it's Darius. Is Lil Mark there?"

My eyes got as big as bagels. Not only did I hate being called Lil Mark, but I absolutely didn't want to talk to him. Before I knew it, I was rapidly shaking my head and mouthing the word, "No!"

"I'm sorry, baby," my mom fibbed. "He's not home right now."

After hanging up, my mom gave me the *who are you and what have you done with my double scoop of dark chocolate* look. "Mark," she said, wiping her hands on her apron. "If you let them into your heart, you'll see that having family is a blessing."

"Sure, if you think constant drama, arguments, and dysfunction are a blessing," I replied, sarcastically.

"You know, blood is thicker than water."

"Well, oil is thicker than both. So, should I start calling the tires on your car my family?"

"You think your real smart don't you. You ain't cute."

We both began to laugh, and she never tried to force the issue. She loved me unconditionally and accepted me for what I was and who I became. But because my mother knew that I wasn't a family person, and she was the biggest family person who ever lived with the biggest blabber mouth, she felt comfortable sharing all the family secrets with me including the people in our family that she loved and the people she loved but really didn't like.

By the time I turned fourteen years old, I had become more introverted and not only disliked being around my family, but also disliked being around people in general. So, my mom enrolled me at Canisius High School during my sophomore year to help me deepen my understanding of God and get me away from the bad crowd I started hanging around with during my freshman year at another high school. To be clear, the only reason I started hanging around with them was because I wasn't challenged academically, and you know what they say: an idle mind is the devil's playground.

When I look back, I really regret the wrong decisions I made at such a young age during my freshman year of high school because transferring from a predominantly Black high school to Canisius was a shock to my system. Canisius High School was an all-boys Catholic school with a population that I swear was ninety-nine percent White. There had to be less than ten Black students in the entire school, and I was one of them.

But shortly after I started attending, I began sharing a locker with Mitch, a dark-skinned brother like me who had a curly 'fro and dimples for days. Knowing that we were two of the very few Black people there, and that we both came from the East side, gave us an instant connection. And as the year progressed, he became my brother from another mother and was the only person, besides my mom, that I enjoyed being around. And when I introduced him to my mom, she instantly loved him and was so happy that I had met a friend that I could relate to and who could relate to me.

Now, I can't remember who it was, but one of us kept a bottle of hot sauce in our locker to spice up our lunches. But one day, when we were standing at our locker talking, Mitch opened the door and the bottle of hot sauce fell to the ground, breaking the glass and splashing hot sauce everywhere. Suddenly, every White person within a twenty-foot radius was staring at us as we stood in a puddle of hot sauce.

At that time, I felt an immediate sense of humiliation. I'm in this all-white school perpetuating the false notion that all Black people had to have hot sauce with them. In hindsight, it was quite humorous, and even to this day, we jokingly believe that the hot sauce bottle belonged to the other person. So, since this is my book, I'm stating for the last time that it was not my damn bottle of hot sauce.

Mitch and I were the best of friends all through high school and had a lot in common when it came to things like playing sports and video games. But when it came to our taste in women, we were lightyears apart.

In Spring of 2007, about a month before graduating from high school, Mitch and I were talking on the phone when his other line rang. "Hold on," he said. "Let me see who this is."

He clicked over to answer the other line as I waited patiently. Two minutes later, he returned. "My boy, this girl I got on the other line, she bad. She'll make you wanna risk it all."

I rolled my eyes. "Negro, please! If she's all that, why aren't you talking to her?"

"Aye bro, don't worry 'bout what I'm doing over here. I already got a lil somethin-somethin' I'm workin' on. Besides, have I ever steered you wrong?"

"Yes!" I quickly answered. "Remember the last girl you said was all that? The one whose thighs and calves connect? What was ol' girl's name? Oh yeah, no knees Brenda, talking 'bout she was Cambridge Avenue's finest!"

"Nah, man, it's not like that," Mitch insisted as he laughed. "Me and Roshneke are just friends, but she fine. You remember the movie *Friday,* right? Ms. Parker—Ms. Parker ain't got nothing on her. Wanna meet her?"

After going back and forth a few more times, I conceded. Seconds later, I was a silent listener on a three-way call, and Roshneke had no idea.

Initially, I wasn't going to say a word—I didn't want to waste her time or mine. But as I listened to her speaking, her voice got to me. Before I knew it, my heart was pounding in my chest, and I definitely wanted to meet her.

I wasn't worried about her liking me 'cause even though I was weird, introverted, and whatever else you wanted to say, I knew one thing and one thing for sure…. At age seventeen, I was *fine* if I do say so myself. I was a six-foot-six, 250-pound double scoop of dark chocolate with game. Let me put it this way. If Tyson Beckford and I walked into a room together…you wouldn't know who's who. Now if y'all thought I wasn't going to gas myself up in my own book, you must have lost your mind.

Under normal conditions, I would've said something smooth to make my presence known and pique Roshneke's interest. But my heart was still pounding, and I couldn't concentrate. So, I did the only thing I could think of—I started barking. Barking like a big dog.

At first, Roshneke ignored me and continued talking to Mitch. So, I barked harder and louder to get her attention.

Suddenly, my bedroom door swung open. "Mark!" my mom yelled, standing in the doorway with a rolling pin in her hand. "Are you insane?"

Roshneke immediately started laughing as I covered the phone. "Go away, mom," I whispered. "I got this girl on the phone."

When I returned to the phone call, Roshneke was still laughing, and I thought all hope was lost. But when Mitch introduced us and she said that my barking was cute, we agreed to meet in person. She said she was bringing her younger sister, Trisha, in case I turned out to be a barking lunatic. We both had a good laugh and met at McDonalds a few hours later. When I saw her standing at the entrance with reddish-brown braids, caramel-colored skin, and curves for days and she saw me standing a foot taller than her and looking dark chocolatey, it was love at first sight and the sparks definitely flew. A few hours later, we were officially dating.

Over the next month, the bond between me and Rosh grew, and I wanted my mom to meet her. She was quickly becoming another woman that I needed in my life, and I had to know if she would get along with my mom.

The next day, I invited Rosh to our house for dinner and from the time she arrived until the time she left, my mom and Rosh were like two extroverted peas in a pod who talked, talked, talked—the whole time. And, I'll be honest, I loved it because talking to each other meant I didn't have to talk; plus, I enjoyed listening to my mom trying to say Rosh's name with her Alabama accent. She never did say it right and always ended up calling her Rosh-neekie.

Rosh and I continued dating after we graduated from high school but ended our relationship amicably in August 2007 before we both went off to college—she was accepted at Howard University in Washington, D.C. and I was accepted at Wayne State University in Detroit, Michigan. I was excited about going off to college and was even more excited to earn a bachelor's degree and make my mom proud.

"Mark, I want you to work hard, get good grades, and earn your degree," my mom said after we packed my last duffle bag. "I know this is your first time living away from home, but don't get distracted."

"Don't worry mom. I got this. Before you know it, I'll have my degree."

My mom gave me a kiss on the cheek. "I know you do. You know I love you."

I smiled. "Thank you, mom," I replied. "I won't let you down."

Afterwards, she took me to the bus station and four hours later, I was in Detroit, Michigan. *Motown baby!* And getting checked into my dorm room on campus at Wayne State.

Now, my intentions were honorable when I left home and headed for college, but you must understand, I was eighteen years old and away from home for the first time ever *in downtown Detroit.* And no matter how hard I tried to stick to my morals and stay focused on school, I couldn't. Not only was I was living in a coed dorm with some of the finest women I'd ever seen, but I had a male roommate who was a complete party animal. And when we became best friends, before I knew it, I was a party animal, too.

During my first semester at Wayne State, my roommate and I partied like rock stars, and I didn't have a shot at staying focused from the start. Hell, the very first night there, a girl in the room next to us ran out of her room topless. "Shots! Shots! Shots!" she screamed with a bottle of Mr. Boston in her hand.

And yes, I took the offer of those shots. That's how the semester started and every day afterwards, my roommate and I played video games, went to sport games, drank a ton of alcohol even though we were underaged, smoked a ton of weed, and even did 'shrooms instead of studying and doing homework. And I couldn't believe how easy it was to get people over twenty-one years of age to buy beer for us. The whole semester, we partied every day, went out all the time, had daily drinking contests, and flirting with college women. I absolutely loved being in Detroit and I had never felt so free and so relaxed in my life.

I had to drop out of college at the end of the first semester because my grades were horrendous. And I can't begin to tell you how disappointed my mom was when I returned to Buffalo and moved back in with her. But I can tell you that the disappointment she felt at that moment was nothing compared to the disappointment she felt over the next two years as I kept returning to Detroit just to party instead of trying to do something with my life.

Eventually, I started dating a young woman in Detroit who was a student at Wayne State. We became friends during my first semester there and when we started dating, she allowed me to secretly live in her dorm room, even though she had a female roommate.

On days when my girlfriend was in class, I hid in her room while her roommate was there. Looking back, I wish I could apologize to the roommate because I can't imagine how she must have felt having this big man there alone with her. Granted, I never came out of the bedroom and had no ill intentions whatsoever, but she didn't know that. So, by any chance if she happens to read this book, I offer you my sincerest apologies. You were put in a position you should never have been in.

Back to the story, though. I was in my early twenties, had a free place to stay with no responsibilities, and was living in the city that I loved drinking and partying my life away and emailing my mother every two weeks asking her to send me money.

Eventually, I got an interview for a job as a door-to-door lawnmower salesman and emailed my mom to share the good news.

A few minutes later, I received her reply.

Mark,

I've done everything I know how to do to be a good mother to you and put you on a path to success. You said you had everything figured out, but you didn't. The only reason you're barely making it in Detroit is because you're using me as your personal ATM asking for $200 every other week. All the money I paid for you to go to Canisius only for you to be happy to be a door-to-door lawnmower salesman ?????

I am so disappointed in you, son.

When I read my mom's email, on the inside it tore me up bad, but on the outside—nothing. No visible signs of sadness. Knowing how bad I was letting my mom down and having her express it to me was all I needed to make a change.

In October 2010, I returned to Buffalo, moved back in with my mom, and renewed my driver's license. And when I discovered a week later that Rosh had returned to Buffalo, too, after Howard University became unaffordable, I was ecstatic. A few days later, we reconnected, and it was love at first sight all over again.

In 2012, I enrolled at Buffalo State University, now Buffalo State College. I was more determined than ever to make something out of my life and was willing to be as committed as it took to earn my degree. And after working hard during the first two years and staying focused, I was well on my way to accomplishing my goal. If only I had known that a major obstacle would appear and threaten to not only derail my education, but also my life.

CHAPTER 3
*Life's a B***H — Nas*

When I started attending Buffalo State University, I began having random seizures out of nowhere and was diagnosed with epilepsy, specifically, partial complex seizures. With these types of seizures, I would have one seizure, but they would be in clusters.

At first, the seizures did not affect my ability to go to class, complete my homework, or work part-time. Eventually, they became disruptive and impacted my ability to work and attend class, even with the medication I was taking which forced me to stop working so that I could focus on my schooling. And although my mom was worried, she was optimistic.

In addition to impacting my ability to work and attend class, the seizures also impacted my ability to drive a car. This was particularly frustrating because I had just renewed my driver's license. Now, I could no longer drive a car because the risk of having a seizure while driving was too high.

Despite the obstacles that were put in my path, I graduated from Buffalo State in 2015 with a double bachelor's degree in urban planning & financial economics. I will always remember walking across the stage

Me standing with my mom after graduating from college

and seeing the smile on my mother's face and knowing that she was proud of me. In that moment, I was on top of the world and my future was looking bright.

But even though I felt like I was on top of the world, physically I was struggling because the seizures I was having were becoming more frequent. Despite this, I managed to secure a job at a Fortune 500 company. With Rosh earning a good salary as a nurse and me having landed a good job at twenty-five years old, I knew it was time for me to leave my mama's nest.

The first month living with Rosh in our new apartment felt like a dream come true as we kept up with paying our rent and utilities. I know bragging about paying rent and utilities isn't always appropriate, but it was a great feeling to be able to pay for things on my own, not having to rely on my mom to pay for things like I did when I lived with her. I felt like a real adult, and I was especially proud to have achieved this milestone as a young black man.

Having my degree, a job, a good woman, and my own place felt like my dreams were becoming reality and that I was finally becoming the man my mother always knew I could be, instead of the person I was in Detroit.

As I previously mentioned, my seizures became increasingly disruptive over time. After a while, I began having seizures about every ten to fourteen days, which usually involved multiple cluster seizures. Following each seizure, I would need to take a couple of weeks off from work to rest and recuperate and because they were happening so often, it didn't take long for companies to tire of paying me a salary when I was absent two weeks out of the month due to my illness.

One thing you should know about me, the emotions I feel on the inside are rarely expressed physically, but that wasn't the case when it came to anger. When I'm angry, the intense emotions that I feel are visible to everyone around me as the people I worked with soon discovered. I remember the day vividly. Four months had passed since the day I began working at this Fortune 500 company and during this time, I had four seizures. The next day, I arrived at my desk to start my 9 a.m. shift as usual. But when I logged into to my computer and opened my email, I saw an email from Human Resources (HR) requesting that I come to their office.

Once I got there, they asked me to take a seat and a few minutes later, three people arrived. Without sugarcoating anything, they said that I was being terminated for violating the attendance policy. I attempted to explain that the missed days were due to my epilepsy and that I had a doctor's note to prove it, but they weren't interested.

As you can imagine, I was furious. And after using some of the colorful language I learned from my mother when she was trying to whoop me at age twelve and throwing what some described as an adult tantrum, I stood outside in a state of shock and waited for the bus to come so I could get home.

When I got home, I was full of so much anger that I walked into the apartment and immediately started punching the wall.

"It's going to be okay," Rosh said, trying to comfort me.

"How is it going to be okay, Rosh? It doesn't matter how hard I work, as soon as the seizures start, I'm out of a job."

"Baby, I know it hurts," she calmly said. "But I know you. And I know you're stronger than this. You will get another job just like you got this one."

I pulled Rosh close to me and held her tight. "You're right. *I am* stronger than this and it's time for me to man up."

Over the next few years, I applied for jobs, went on interviews, and explained to employers that I have epilepsy. And I would either get hired, but then get fired due to missed time, or not get hired at all because with two bachelor's degrees I was overqualified for an entry-level position.

I remember the time I was let go that hurt me the most. I believe this was in 2017. I was working for a temp agency that had placed me in a financial institution, which had the potential to hire me on a full-time basis. By this time, medical marijuana had been legalized in the state of New York which meant that employers couldn't fire you for testing positive. However, since the financial institution I was working at dealt with federal matters, it was up to their discretion.

Seven months had passed since the day I began working at this financial institution through the temp agency when a position opened that I was encouraged to apply for. I applied for the position and during the interview process, informed the interviewers that I had epilepsy, had been prescribed medical marijuana, and would test positive if I was given a drug test. At that time, I was assured by the Vice President of the company that this wouldn't be a problem and that I would still be hired.

On what was supposed to be my official first day working for them instead of the temp agency, I was called into a meeting by the same Vice President and assumed it was to do more paperwork, but I was wrong. When I arrived, an HR representative introduced herself and I noticed that the Vice President's eyes were glossy, as if he had been crying. Moments later, the position I was offered was rescinded because I tested positive for medical marijuana and I was fired, effective immediately.

At that point, I just felt tired, numb, and emotionless and wanted to get home. As I was leaving the office, the Vice President called out my name and begged me to stop. He was crying and apologizing profusely, stating that he had been fighting for me to keep the job, but HR and the institution wouldn't allow it. I'll be honest, I didn't care whether he had been fighting for me or against me, I was just numb and felt no empathy or sympathy for him.

Without saying a word, I walked out the door to catch the bus home and felt like a hamster running on a hamster wheel and getting nowhere. Once home, I found myself instantly becoming depressed and thinking dangerous thoughts. *My degrees are worthless. My life is worthless. Maybe I should just kill myself and call it a wrap.*

Over the next two weeks, I continued spiraling downward and having dark thoughts about the various ways I could end this wretched thing called life. *Maybe I should overdose on my epilepsy medication or jump in front of an oncoming train. Maybe I should leap into Niagara Falls or from the top of a building downtown.*

And even though I knew that I would never commit suicide, it gave me a little comfort thinking about it. I never told my mom or Rosh this. I didn't feel like worrying them with these dark thoughts I was having. I didn't want to scare them or make them worry about me more than they already did.

Because I couldn't succeed in a career based on my field of study, I started working dead-end jobs over the next several years. And as if that wasn't bad enough, watching Rosh advance in her career and assume responsibility for eighty percent of our bills added insult to injury. Don't get me wrong, I wanted her to succeed, but I didn't feel worthy of being a man. I felt like I was having another woman take care of me, once again, since I couldn't take care of myself.

It was also hard watching my friends and peers earning double if not triple the amount of money that I was making and advancing in their careers while I was stuck with no hope of advancing in mine. But I decided not to sulk and began to accept and make the most of the hand I was dealt.

Fortunately for me, through God's grace, the right medication, or whatever, at the end of 2018 my epilepsy just went away, and the next two years of my life were amazing. In 2020, Rosh and I said our "I do's" at the courthouse and officially became husband and wife; and I got off the hamster wheel and started working at Erie County Medical Center (ECMC) as a Patient Access Service Representative. And even though it wasn't my ideal job, I worked hard and did my best.

My hard work paid off because in November 2021, I became a Public Safety Assistant. Words can't describe how great it felt to finally earn enough money to contribute to our household financially. More importantly, I felt as if I had a new career, and my future was looking brighter than ever.

Over the next year and a half, Rosh and I spent a lot of time doing couples things with my mom and her new boyfriend Malcolm. I loved Malcolm, we got along perfectly. We both were very low-key people. But most importantly, Malcolm was a hard worker. He worked two jobs and over sixty hours a week. And after watching my mom go from one trashy boyfriend wreaking of alcohol to another trashy boyfriend who couldn't keep a job to save his life, it felt great seeing her with someone who was worthy of her and everything she had to offer.

As 2021 ended, I was confident that 2022 was going to be the best year yet for me, on a career level, and Rosh as well since she was now a nurse practitioner. But in the middle of March, Rosh began struggling to stay awake while she worked her shift. She had never experienced that level of fatigue before and assumed that it was due to a lack of water. But when she missed her period a few days later, she suspected that it was something else and secretly took an at-home pregnancy test as I played video games in the living room.

"Talley, come here!" she yelled.

I put down the controller and walked into the bathroom. "What's up?"

Rosh was smiling so big I could barely see her eyes. "We're having a baby, Talley!" she said, showing me the double lines on the pregnancy test.

"Welp, guess I better stop buying video games," I joked.

When Rosh told me that she was pregnant, on the inside I was excited about being a dad, but on the outside—nothing. No visible signs of excitement.

"I'm so happy, baby!" Rosh replied as tears of joy filled her eyes. Can you believe it? We're going to be parents!"

I hugged her tightly. "Time to stop all this crying and man up," I joked.

On March 12th, we called my mom on speaker to share the good news.

"Mom," I calmly said, "Rosh is pregnant."

"Are you serious?" she asked, her country accent sounding strong. "You know how much I want a grandchild. Are you serious?"

"I'm serious," I calmly replied.

"Don't get me excited for nothing, Mark. You know I want to be a grandma. Are you really serious?"

"I'm not going to keep saying this, now," I chuckled.

"Rosh-neekie?" she called out, mispronouncing Rosh's name yet again. "Is he joking? You know he's a jokester."

"He's not joking, mama G. I'm really pregnant."

The next thing I knew, my mom was screaming at the top of her lungs, and I could hear the excitement in her voice. "We're having a baby!" she cried out. "Oh, thank you Lord! We're having a baby!"

For the next eight weeks, my mom was happier than I'd ever seen and was exhibiting typical grandparent behavior—you know, buying things for the baby, calling to check on Rosh regularly, and telling everyone she knew that she was going to be a first-time grandma.

But on the morning of May 7th, one day before Mother's Day, the happiness that Rosh and I had been feeling over the last eight weeks abruptly came to an end when she woke up, saw blood in her underwear and in the toilet, and realized that she had a miscarriage. Prior to this, we had made plans to visit both of our mothers on Mother's Day, but now Rosh was too distraught to celebrate, especially since she was no longer going to be a mother herself. And because we didn't want the loss of our baby to overshadow our mothers' special holiday, we decided to postpone telling them for a week and decided that we would visit each of our mothers when I got off work on May 14th. If only I had known that Rosh and I would never have a chance to tell my mom that we lost the baby.

CHAPTER 4

Feel It in The Air – Beanie Sigel

The alarm clock on my nightstand went off loudly at 4 a.m. When I awoke, I assumed May 14th was just another Saturday here in Buffalo. After rubbing the sleep from my eyes and turning off the beeping alarm, I propped myself up on one elbow and watched Rosh as she slept with a blanket covering her body that conformed to her curves. Fifteen years had passed since I first laid eyes on her, but she was still as beautiful as ever. And when I thought about the day the sound of her voice had me barking like a dog, a gentle smile crept up my face and I felt like the luckiest man in the world.

The last seven days had been particularly hard on Rosh. After miscarrying our baby, she began experiencing phantom pregnancy symptoms and fell into depression, barely eating any food or getting any sleep. As I laid in bed watching her, it did my heart good to see her finally getting some rest.

41

She must've sensed me watching her because she slowly opened her eyes. "What are you doing?" she asked, with a slight smile.

"Admiring your short self." I leaned over and kissed her lips gently. "How are you feeling?"

"A little better—I think."

"That's good. I was giving you two more days," I chuckled. "Then you were going to have to man up."

"Whatever Talley. And I'm not short!" she grinned, crossing her arms. "Five-six is above-average for a woman."

"I'm a foot taller than you, so above-average or not—you're still short. A half-pint of caramel in my gallon of dark chocolate. A teaspoon of jelly in my jar of peanut butter. A quart of—"

"Whatever Talley," she laughed. "Don't forget—we're going to your mom's house when you get off work. We can't put off telling her we lost the baby. It'll just be harder on her."

When she said that we were going to my mom's house after work to tell her that we lost the baby, I thought I was going to be sick. I knew we agreed to tell her today, but now I wished we had ripped the band-aid off and told her immediately after it happened. If we did, I wouldn't be feeling sick about telling her when I got off work today.

I sighed and gave Rosh another gentle kiss. "Try not to wake Porkchop," she said. "If you do, you'll have to take her outside."

"I won't wake her. I got this."

Porkchop was our bulldog who was sleeping in the hallway outside of our room. Rosh had always wanted a puppy and after months and months of trying to get me to become a fur dad, I finally gave in.

I climbed out of bed and into the cold of our apartment as goosebumps formed on my arms and legs. Then, with cat-like precision, I tiptoed across the room like a thief in the night carefully avoiding squeaky parts of the floor.

I was halfway to the door when I caught a glimpse of myself in the closet mirror that stopped me in my tracks. *What the hell?* I thought to myself as Rosh giggled from the bed. *I don't look like a thief with cat-like precision—I look like a six-foot-six, 280-pound, dreadlocks-wearing ballerina!*

I shuddered and tried to shake the image from my head. Then I slowly opened the door, tiptoed down the hallway past Porkchop who was still sound asleep, and went into the bathroom to begin my morning triple 'S' effect—you know, shit, shower, and shave. Fifteen minutes later, I returned to my room, got dressed for work, and kissed Rosh goodbye before going outside to wait for my Uber.

As I mentioned earlier, I'm an introvert and from as far back as I can remember, I've never enjoyed making small talk with strangers, and I've never enjoyed it when strangers made small talk with me. But over the years, I've discovered that many Uber drivers feel compelled to strike up a conversation with me—you know, saying things like:

Where you from?

What do you do?

Where are you going?

How's the weather?

And I'll be honest, every time it happened, it annoyed the crap out of me. So, when the Uber driver pulled up smiling so wide, I could see his teeth, I instantly knew he was a talker, and it wouldn't be long before he started making small talk with me. So, I hopped in the car and immediately put on my big ass headphones with speakers the size of two cereal bowls. I called them my *Don't Talk to Mee'z*. I called them that hoping the driver would clearly see that my ears, and half of my face, were covered and thus wouldn't be tempted to talk to me. This method worked like a charm for me ninety percent of the time, and I hoped it would work this time, too.

But when I saw his lips moving as he watched me through the rear-view mirror, I knew he belonged to the ten percent group and was eagerly awaiting my response. Maybe it's just me, but I don't get it. If you see somebody wearing these big headphones and the music playing through the speakers is loud enough for you to hear, why would you try to make small talk knowing the person can't hear you?

When I didn't respond to anything he was saying, he eventually got the hint, and I enjoyed a nice talk-free ride to work zoning out to some Jay-Z.

Ten minutes later, we arrived at ECMC where I worked and I had one thing on my mind: Tim Hortons, where lines are long, espresso is king, and the bagel replaced the donut as my breakfast of choice. And after ordering the usual: a double shot of espresso and a bagel with *light* strawberry cream cheese and receiving back a double shot of espresso with a bagel *swallowed* by strawberry cream cheese, I headed to the Behavioral Health wing to begin my shift as a Public Safety Assistant also known as a PSA or—as the patients called us — fake ass security officers.

The Behavioral Health wing housed psychiatric patients; patients with a mental illness; patients put on a psychiatric code because they either drank too much the night before, smoked the wrong substance, stopped taking their medication, or didn't take their mood stabilizer; and basically anyone else who either checked themselves in or were brought in by authorities. As a PSA, it was my responsibility to protect these patients from themselves and other patients, in addition to protecting the staff.

I arrived in the Behavioral Health wing at 6 a.m. to begin my shift and, as usual, everyone else who also worked the first shift was already there and talking to people in their cliques. As I waited for my supervisor to arrive and assign me to my unit, I saw my man, Willie, nodding off. Willie was a supervisor in his mid-thirties and was someone that I enjoyed talking to because he acted like the stereotypical old Black uncle at the BBQ—you know, the one that's always talking nonsense and gibberish to his children and younger nieces and nephews.

I didn't want Willie to get in trouble for falling asleep on the job, so to help him stay awake, I did what I always did. I started joking with him. "Old man," I said out loud. "I hope you're getting this rest so you can see me out on the basketball court because I don't want no excuses when I whoop that ass."

Willie's head popped up like he received a shot of adrenaline. "Your height and size don't mean squat," he laughed. "You don't want none of this."

I chuckled, "There's no way you could see me on the court. You're too short. Too chubby, plus you know when I put that elbow in your chest, you're going to fall over and start wheezing. Even my mama can kick that ass on the court."

Willie stood up as he laughed heartily. "The bigger you are, the harder you gonna fall when I put that ass to the ground, son. If—if you want to learn some stuff, you can come see me whenever and wherever."

Willie and I continued having fun cracking on each other as a few other people in our vicinity laughed. Neither one of us took anything seriously, we just had a good time playing around like we always did.

A few minutes later, my supervisor came in and assigned me and two other PSAs named Matthew and Zeke to the Comprehensive Psychiatric Emergency Program wing in Behavioral Health called CPEP. Consider CPEP as the emergency room for Behavioral Health. For example, if you had a cold or some other physical injury, you would go to the emergency room. Similarly, if you are feeling mentally unwell or suffering from a mental illness, you would come to CPEP.

Now, the reason the supervisor selected Matthew, Zeke, and me to work in CPEP was because we were the biggest men working that shift and had what I called the triple 'M' effect: masculinity, mustaches, and muscles. Matthew was six-five—250 pounds; Zeke was six-one—300 pounds; and like I said earlier, I was six-six—280 pounds. Because of our sizes, our supervisor was confident that we could physically handle situations involving violent and aggressive patients, and he was right. But sometimes we got hurt in the process. I've had a mild concussion, head trauma, and a bunch of bumps and bruises, so far.

We arrived in CPEP looking like the defensive line for the Buffalo Bills wearing our uniforms consisting of black shirts, tan khaki pants, and puffy black jackets that looked like something the Michelin man would wear. One thing to keep in mind about working in CPEP regardless of the position: if you're not okay with your own mental health, you'll struggle with working here because of the horrible stories you'll hear from patients. I'll never forget the day an eleven-year-old girl told me that her mother trafficked her for money up and down the east coast. It was so horrifying hearing her account.

But in addition to hearing horrifying stories, I also experienced some of the funniest things. Now, I knew I wasn't supposed to find humor in behavioral health but given the fact that I had my own mental health issues, and the fact that some of the circumstances were just plain funny, it wasn't hard to break down and laugh, because, after all, I'm human.

The funniest thing I witnessed working in CPEP, was a woman acting hysterical who was brought in with her baby. She appeared to be having some type of psychiatric breakdown and the medical staff and I were trying to take the baby away from her.

After a few minutes, we were able to get the baby away safely. Then, she became even more unhinged and began acting even more berserk. Thankfully, we were finally able to get her medically sedated and put her into another room. Then, we tossed her baby into a plastic bag and put it in the storage room.

Now, you're probably thinking that what we did was criminal, but trust me, if you were there and saw us taking this plastic, Black baby doll away from this White woman who had bags of Enfamil and diapers with her—you would've laughed, too.

Not only did I hear horrifying stories working in CPEP and experience the funniest things, but I also saw things that I wish I could unsee. Disgusting things from the worse patients to deal with in behavioral health—young females. I'll never forget the day that I was assigned to work in the children's unit of CPEP where a young female, around the age of twelve or thirteen was going through puberty and behaving erratically. Suddenly, she reached down into her pants, pulled out a tampon covered in blood, and threw it at me and the staff. Fortunately, I was smart enough to duck, but the person behind me—

well, unfortunately, he didn't. And when that tampon hit him square in the face, I almost vomited and so did he.

Now, I don't want to paint the hospital or CPEP in a bad light because I definitely enjoyed working in Behavioral Health. The staff members were amazing, and there was never a dull moment as we helped patients from all walks of life get their lives back on the right track. So, like I said, I was excited to start my shift because I knew it was going to be another busy but exciting day.

But on May 14th, nothing I was expecting to happen occurred. It was a chill, relaxing, and boring day which was weird, like something out of the twilight zone. And all I did for literally eight and a half hours was sit in CPEP doing a bunch of nothing and anxiously waiting for my shift to end.

At 2:25 p.m., five minutes before my shift was scheduled to end, everyone around me became glued to their cell phones simultaneously. It was weird, like something out of a sci-fi flick. Everyone was glued to their phones like pod people, and it seemed like I was the only one who wasn't. Seconds later, rumors about an active shooting situation began spreading around CPEP. I wasn't concerned about anyone in my family being in the vicinity of an active shooter because there were plenty of shootings in Buffalo over the years, but they never impacted anyone I knew or loved.

At 2:27 p.m., Robert, my other brother from another mother, sent a group text to me and my high school bro, Mitch. Robert was married to

Rosh's younger sister, Trisha. And when we met over a decade ago during a double date between me and Rosh and him and Trisha, we instantly hit it off and have been bros' ever since.

When I saw the group text, I immediately opened it since everyone around me was still glued to their phones.

"hey y'all, there's been a shooting," Robert said.

"where?" I asked.

"at Tops on Jefferson," Mitch replied.

Tops Friendly Market was a grocery store located on the east side of Buffalo in a predominantly Black, low socioeconomic neighborhood with its fair share of violent crime.

Although the three of us were born and raised on the east side, we were always quick to make jokes. Nevertheless, I was quick to push back against those who made jokes about my neighborhood without ever having stepped foot in it or lived in it.

So, when Mitch mentioned that the shooting occurred at Tops on Jefferson, we assumed it was just people behaving foolishly, taking advantage of the fine weather after the pandemic. We thought that perhaps people were happy to be able go outside again and that it wasn't anything too serious. "Man, you know its summertime now. Grown folks out here shootin lmao," I texted.

"Nah, bruh, it's the young ass kids shooting shit up," Robert replied.

I chimed back in and started clowning with Robert. "Robert, man, shut yo old ass up lol, sounding like an old ass man."

Robert texted back. "Worry about not getting yo head knocked off by a patient lol."

We continued clowning around with each other in our group text, completely unaware of how serious the situation at Tops really was.

A few minutes later, my relief arrived, my shift finally ended, and I couldn't wait to leave the hospital. And although I wasn't looking forward to telling my mother that we lost the baby, I was looking forward to seeing her. If only I had known that I would never see her again.

CHAPTER 5
Crazy – Gnarles Barkley

I exited the hospital through the main entrance and was glad to see Rosh waiting in the car for me. I opened the car door, jumped into the passenger seat, and leaned over to give her a kiss.

"Baby, there's been a shooting at Tops," she said with an unsteady voice. "It's all over the radio. I called my mom and Trisha. They weren't there, thank goodness. I hope no one else we know is there."

I didn't want to hear any news about the active shooting situation, so I connected my phone to the car's Bluetooth to listen to music. "I doubt anyone we know is there. Besides dudes get shot everyday B," I chuckled, reciting a line from the movie *Paid in Full*.

"Ready to go see your mom?"

"Yeah, but let's go home first. I want to take off this uniform and grab a bite to eat."

Rosh tucked her braids behind her ears and started driving us home. Normally, I would've been telling her all about the craziness that happened at work, but like I said, it was a pretty chill and relaxed day. So instead of talking, I held her hand and dozed off listening to music as Porkchop slept on the backseat.

We made it home at 2:45 p.m. and Porkchop immediately ran to her food bowl in the kitchen. Rosh followed me into the bedroom and sat down on the edge of the bed as I put my cell phone on the dresser. "I checked on my mom," she said. "Don't you think you should check on your mom?"

When I heard her question, I kind of lashed out—not angrily, just sort of nonchalantly. "What do you mean check on her?"

She raised her eyebrows. "They're. Shooting. At. Tops," she said, putting emphasis on each word. "Don't you want to make sure she's not there?"

"For what?" I shrugged my shoulders in confusion as I stood in front of the open closet door. "Why on earth would my mom be at Tops today? It's Saturday. Malcolm takes her to the lake every Saturday then they go home. She's okay. She's good. Ain't nothing wrong."

Rosh stood up and sighed. "You're right, baby. We haven't done anything to deserve that kind of pain on top of everything else we've been through. And she doesn't even live near Tops anymore."

Rosh walked out the door as I removed my puffy black jacket and hung it in the closet. Then, I walked over to the bed, without a care in the world. But before I had a chance to sit down, Rosh's words hit me hard, like a lightning bolt to my chest.

> *They're shooting at Tops. Don't you want to make sure she's not there?*

I sat down on the edge of the bed as a whirlwind of thoughts ripped through my mind. *Mom is with Malcolm, they're probably on their way home from the lake. She's not at Tops right now. She knows it's too crowded.*

I continued reasoning with myself as I stared at my phone still sitting on the dresser. And when I finally concluded that it was better to call and verify that she was safe than not call and find out later that she wasn't, I grabbed my phone, sat back down on the bed, and dialed her number. The call connected and kept ringing until it went to voicemail.

I wasn't convinced that anything was wrong when she didn't answer. I just assumed that she and Malcolm were still at the lake. I did want to make sure they knew about the active shooter situation, so I dialed his number. It didn't even ring. It just went straight to voicemail.

I leaned forward with my elbows on my knees and my phone in my hand and ran through the possible reasons neither one of them were answering their phones. *Maybe they're on a romantic getaway and don't want to be disturbed. Maybe they got a hotel somewhere and put their phones on silent. Maybe their playing hide the salami and—Nooo!* I shook my head, trying to erase the image. *Wrong thought! Wrong thought!*

Suddenly, Rosh walked into our room with her phone in hand. "Your family is messaging me on Facebook," she said. "They said they're trying to call you, but they keep getting your voicemail."

"Yeah, my phone's is on do not disturb."

"Is that's a good idea? What if your mom calls?"

"It's all good. She'll still be able to reach me. You can also call me and get through if my phone is on do not disturb."

"So, do you want me to tell them you're not here?"

"No," I replied as I took my phone off do not disturb. "Tell them to try calling me now."

I always had my phone on do not disturb so I could avoid unnecessary calls and because one of my biggest pet peeves is when someone calls and when I answer the first thing they say is, *'whatchu doing?'* I hate that. I hate it with a passion. It's like people want to be nosey and pry into your business. There's no reason for the call except to ask that and I don't get it. What is the point of calling someone and asking what they're doing? And that's all. That's it. That's the whole reason for the call. I even hate it when Rosh does it. The only person I was OK with doing it was my mom because…she's mom.

Me personally, I would never call someone and ask what they're doing—I mean, if I call you, I'm going to go from point A to point Z as quickly as possible, with no filler information because I like my calls like I liked my Burnettes back in my younger years—straight no chaser.

As you can tell by the alcohol choice I referenced, I was 'broke phi broke' in my early twenties.

Unfortunately, the people in my family are notorious for calling and asking me what I'm doing, that's why I kept my phone on do not disturb.

After Rosh replied to the messages she received, my phone immediately rang. It was my niece, Laura. I figured she was calling to say that my mom was with her or my sister.

I answered the call on speaker and immediately heard sirens, screaming, and sobbing in the background, as Laura cried hysterically. Rosh's eyes filled with tears as she looked at me and I looked back at her. Neither one of us said a word, we just waited for my niece to calm down enough to speak.

"Mark, this is Laura," she said, in between sniffles. "I'm at Tops. Police are everywhere—there's been a—a shooting. I-I don't know how to say this—but your mom is inside. Malcolm is here, too. He's freaking out, Mark. He said they were separated when the shooting started but now, he's outside and we can't find her. And they're not letting anyone inside. We're trying to get more information, but can you come down?"

Rosh began crying hysterically as I stared at the phone. "Yeah, I'll be there."

From the moment that my phone rang, I had a sick feeling in my gut telling me that my mom was dead. I don't know how to describe it except to say that when I answered Laura's call, it felt like a roller coaster inside my stomach began moving slowly up an invisible track. When I heard all that crying and screaming, the roller coaster and fear of the unknown gained momentum inside me. And when she said that my mother was there and they couldn't find her, the roller coaster reached the highest point, then plunged into darkness. I felt numbness everywhere. In my heart I knew that my mom didn't make it out of Tops, especially with her bad knees. We always joked about which one of us would need knee surgery first.

After hanging up the phone, Rosh jumped up in a panic. "We've got to go, Mark," she insisted, grabbing her purse, keys, and sweater.

I didn't budge. I just—you know, felt frozen.

When Rosh called me Mark, I knew she was scared. She loved my mom as much as she loved her own mother. Looking back, I wish I had been capable of understanding her emotions and what she was going through. But I wasn't moving at a snail's pace on purpose. I wouldn't do that to Rosh or my mom. I was just in a state of shock—not mentally, but physically. And, like I said, I got a feeling in my gut that my mom was dead. So, in my mind there was no need to rush because she was already gone.

After getting undressed and tossing my work clothes in the hamper, I was stinky but still decided to put on a black hoodie, gray sweatpants, and my black air forces. A few minutes later, Rosh and I made it to the car. But as soon as she started to drive, I found myself thinking about the horrors awaiting me at Tops. So, I closed my eyes and tried to focus on something pleasant. And because I had been awake since 4 a.m., it didn't take long for my mind to drift into daydreaming about the day I discovered that my mom was big into horoscopes.

She was sitting at the kitchen table drinking a cup of lemon water and flipping pages in the newspaper.

"There's my double scoop of dark chocolate," she said as I walked up and sat down at the table with her.

I smiled. "What are you doing?"

"Reading my horoscope. I read it every day."

"What the heck are horoscopes. I asked. "Does dad read his horoscope?"

"No, baby," she chuckled. "Your dad doesn't read his horoscope."

"You can read me my horoscope if you want."

My mom's eyes lit up like sparklers on the Fourth of July. "Well, Mark," she excitedly said. "The first thing you need to know is that your personality is part Cancer and part Gemini."

Then, she proceeded to read my horoscope for that day, and I actively listened to every word she read.

When she finished, she looked up from her newspaper and saw me grinning like a Cheshire cat. "What do you think of your horoscope?" She asked before taking a sip of lemon water.

> *"Well mom, I think you're too old to be reading this magical nonsense."*
>
> *Suddenly, my mom burst into laughter and started spitting lemon water all over me and my horoscope!*

As I continued daydreaming about my mom, a peace came over me. That is, until I opened my eyes and saw how close we were to Tops. And when that roller coaster feeling I had inside me returned, I realized that Tops was the last place on earth I wanted to be.

One reason I didn't want to be at Tops was because I was certain that, by now, every family member I had on this side of New York was there and I didn't want to be around any of them. Another reason I didn't want to be at Tops was because I couldn't handle being around a large crowd of high emotions people. And I already knew that my family, along with many other people, would be there crying, hollering, trying to give me hugs, and trying to hold and touch me and I don't like to be touched. Now, I don't mind Rosh touching and holding me. Didn't mind my mom doing it, either. But anyone else? Hell nah! I would rather shit in a hat and wear it on my head than have someone else touching me. I just can't do it. Plus, the introvert in me can't handle being around all that screaming, crying, and hollering.

But the biggest reason I didn't want to be at Tops was because I didn't want to see the policemen. I didn't want to see the reporters. I didn't want to see the ambulances. And, most importantly, I didn't want to deal with the noise. I just didn't want to be there.

I glanced at Rosh in the driver's seat and saw tears in her eyes as she sped trying to get to Tops as fast as she could. While she drove, I stared out the windshield at the aging buildings along the way and was calm, cool, and collected—on the outside, that is. On the inside, I was having some kind of meltdown as each block we passed brought us closer to confirmation that my mother was dead, something I just didn't think I was mentally ready to receive. I mean—it's one thing to have a gut feeling that your mom is dead, but it's an entirely different story to confirm it.

We were three blocks away from Tops and minutes away from the chaos and the confirmation that I mentally could not handle receiving. Suddenly, I saw the Tops Friendly Market signage in the distance and broke out in a cold sweat. "Rosh, pull over," I calmly said.

"Baby, we're almost there."

"Stop the car. Just pull over."

She pulled over to the curb and put the car in park. "Are you okay?"

I couldn't look Rosh in the eyes, so I continued staring out the windshield. "I don't want to go to Tops. I'm not trying to be at that circus with my family—I mean, I don't want to be near them when things are good, so why would I go there to be with them now?"

Rosh took a deep breath and gently grabbed my hand. "I know

you're scared. I'm scared, too. But, baby, we're not going to Tops for them. We're going to Tops for your mom and for Malcolm."

"My mom is dead, Rosh."

"You don't know that. Laura said—"

"She's dead. I can feel it in my gut, and I can't be in that chaotic environment right now. And I can't handle seeing Malcolm right now.

Tears streamed down Rosh's cheeks. I didn't want her to cry, so I gently wiped the tears from her eyes, licked my lips as part of my best LL Cool J impression, and tried to make her laugh. "Rosh, you need to man up," I said, sarcastically.

Rosh didn't respond, but she didn't have to. The rage in her eyes and steam coming out of her ears said it all. Oh well. Sometimes you take a chance and try to make someone laugh, and sometimes you end up with an angry woman wanting to punch you in the face.

As Rosh continued to cry, I knew she was struggling with the hard decision she had to make—either going to Tops out of love for my mom, or not going to Tops out of love for me. Nonetheless, this was only the beginning of this painful nightmare.

CHAPTER 6
So Many Tears – Tupac Shakur

As Rosh sat in the driver's seat wrestling with the decision she had to make, I sat in the passenger seat trying to wrap my head around how drastically things changed from the time I left the hospital at 2:30 p.m.—I mean, one minute I was planning to visit my mother after work, and the next minute I was facing the stark possibility of planning her funeral. And I knew Rosh was frustrated with me and my decision not to go to Tops, but I also knew she understood.

After talking it through a little more, Rosh called her younger sister, Trisha, to brief her on the situation with my mom and let her know that we were on our way. Trisha was five months pregnant and was having a gender reveal party at 7 p.m., so she already knew we were coming over. But what she didn't know was that we would be coming four hours early. I knew she and Robert wouldn't mind, though. With everything going on with my mom, I knew that being in their company would help.

We arrived at Robert and Trisha's apartment complex at about 3:30 p.m. and as soon as we parked the car, my phone rang. It was my family calling to find out when I was coming to Tops. I didn't want to deal with anyone, so I didn't answer. Then, I started receiving more and more calls from family members, one after another. I didn't want to deal with them either, so I ignored their calls, too.

As we walked to the apartment building from the parking lot, I gave my phone to Rosh because the constant calls coming in from my family were causing me to stress. Then, we took the elevator to the fifth floor and walked down the hallway to Robert and Trisha's apartment.

We opened the unlocked door and walked out of the hallway and into the apartment which was covered in pink and blue decorations. There were pink and blue streamers across the ceiling and walls, pink and blue balloons scattered everywhere, a pink and blue three-tier cake on the dining table, along with pink and blue plates, cups, and eating utensils. There were also two gold balloons in the middle of the room—one filled with pink confetti, and the other filled with blue confetti.

Immediately after greeting everyone, Rosh joined her mom and sister in the kitchen as they cooked food for the party, and I dapped up Robert before sitting down on the couch.

"What's going on, man? You straight?" Robert asked before taking a sip of Cîroc.

"You know—it is what it is."

Robert knew I had a lot of things weighing heavily on my mind, but he also knew what to say to distract me. "Remember that time we tried to see who could drink the most tallboys?"

I chuckled. "Who could forget?"

For the next twenty or so minutes, Robert and I reminisced about the drinking game we played ten years ago to see who could drink the most Silver Thunder tallboys before passing out. Silver Thunder was the worst of the worst malt liquor as far as I was concerned, but after drinking two of them each, neither one of us had passed out. So, to speed things up, we drank a few shots of Mr. Boston, too.

"You should've seen yourself stumbling to the bathroom," I laughed. "You barely made it to the toilet before you threw up, stumbled back to the couch, and threw up again all over yourself before passing out. I had to carry your heavy butt to the shower while the girls washed vomit off you and your clothes!"

After Trish, Rosh, and I dragged Robert's confused and dazed butt to the bed to lay down, I couldn't wait to tease him the next day and tell him that I won. But suddenly, I had an intense urge to puke. So, I covered my mouth with my hand to hold it in, ran to the bathroom, and dropped to my knees before spewing vomit in the toilet, on the toilet, on the floor, and on my chest and arms. Then, I passed out in my own vomit.

"Seriously, bro, I still don't know how Rosh and Trisha dragged you out of the bathroom and put you in the bed with me," Robert laughed.

"You're a foot taller than Rosh and even taller than Trisha! And you're definitely bigger than both!"

"You got that right!" I laughed. "I felt like a giant in tiny town standing next to our wives! But all joking aside, we were some wild boys in our twenties."

"Yeah, we were," Robert agreed. "Remember the time we called ourselves having a drinking contest because we wanted to see who could take the most shots of—what was it? Oh yeah, Devil's Springs?"

We both started laughing hard. "Man, the contest ended almost as quickly as it started!" I exclaimed. "After three shots, both of us passed out and didn't remember a thing!"

Robert and I continued reminiscing and laughing about our youth gone wild days which was very effective in distracting me from the horrors of the day. That is, until someone knocked on the door.

"It's unlocked," Robert yelled from the couch.

"What's up y'all?" Mitch asked as he walked in. "I could hear y'all laughing all the way down the hall!"

"Nothing much, man." I replied. "Just remembering how wild we were in our twenties."

Robert stood up. "Time for the cave ya'll boys."

We walked down the hall and entered Robert's man cave a few minutes later. Robert immediately sat down on the couch and poured himself a glass of Hennessy. Mitch sat down next to him and popped the cap on a Corona, as I plopped into the recliner and started rolling one up. A few minutes later, I fired it up and took the first two hits before passing it to Robert. But even with all the distractions, I was struggling as the gut feeling inside my stomach telling me my mom was dead played tug-of-war with the pain in my heart hoping she was alive.

Now, I stopped drinking alcohol immediately after I was diagnosed with epilepsy all those years ago. But considering everything that was going on, I made an exception and helped myself to two shots of Hennessy.

Robert passed it to Mitch who immediately took two puffs. Mitch knew me as well as Robert did if not more, and even though I tried to hide it, he could tell that I was still struggling. So, after passing it back to me, he started roasting me about my sneakers to take my mind off my mom. "Mark, man, why you keep wearing your sneakers after they start talking?"

After taking two more puffs, I passed it to Robert. "Because it's expensive as hell to buy size seventeens. And they may be talking, but you're out of shape. I bet you a hundred dollars right now that if you tried to do ten pushups, you couldn't make it to three."

"Y'all both need to join the old man club like me," Robert said after taking two hits. "I'm about to be a father now. I ain't got time to try and partake in y'all nonsense."

Mitch's plan to distract me worked like a charm because we kept roasting each other and talking mega trash. And when tempers started to flare like they always did when we roasted each other, I knew it was time to settle our beefs. "Put the Madden on and let's go then since you acting like you a boss!" I taunted with a smirk.

Madden had been the go-to video game for settling our beefs for over a decade, since neither one of them could play 2K. Only two of us could play at a time, and when we played, we were nasty-competitive and definitely hit below the belt.

My mom hated that I still played video games with a passion. The thing is, I never once got on her about all the lottery tickets she played, but that's another story.

For the next three hours, we acted more like high school teenagers than adults in our thirties as we drank, smoked, and played video games. And every time one of us made a play, the other player yelled, cussed, and accused the game of cheating while the one observing the game tried to gas us up, saying things like, "How you gonna let him do you like that?"

In the middle of drinking, smoking, and playing Madden, I started scrolling through my phone. That's when I realized that the Tops shooter was arrested and taken into custody.

"Mitch, man, you looking kinda pregnant. When's the gender reveal for you happening?" I asked, trying to take my mind off the shooter and get a rise out of Mitch.

Mitch dropped his game controller on the table. "Boy I know yo' fat jiggly puff fat ass ain't talking."

Robert and Mitch busted out laughing as I rolled my eyes.

You probably already know that nothing is more fun than getting on the nerves of your best friends and, at this point, we were all more than friends. We were family in my eyes.

"I got something for y'all," Mitch said, narrowing his eyes at us. "Break out the dice. Let's see if you can put your money where your mouth is!"

We all stood up, acting big and bad as we left the man cave and headed to the living room where Rosh, Mitch's wife, and about seven other guests were doting over Trisha and playing a gender reveal game.

We walked into the living room, and I gave Rosh a hug. "Your family finally stopped calling," she said.

"Did you answer any of their calls?" I asked.

"No, I didn't really know what to say."

Then Robert immediately pulled out the dice from the entertainment center as our wives shook their heads and made their disappointment known in no uncertain terms.

As we got ready to roll the dice, I asked Trisha to turn the music up. I wanted things to be upbeat and lively because everyone was aware of what I was going through, and I didn't want my grief to overshadow Robert and Trisha's celebration.

The party got going again, and Robert, Mitch, and I continued drinking and smoking. "What's bank?" Robert asked.

"Y'all were talking all that ying yang, so I'm setting bank," Mitch chuckled.

"Well set it then," I replied, chuckling too.

Mitch grinned. "Alright. Bank is six dollars."

We each slammed two dollars on the table. Then, the trash talk between us escalated as we prepared to play Cee-lo, a dice game. If you know you know.

I grabbed the dice from the table and was confident about my chances of winning and eager to play with a swag I called my Detroit Swag. A few minutes later, round one of Cee-lo began. All eyes were on me as I walked across the room, leaned back against the wall, and struck a GQ pose with one foot propped up behind me. And when I made eye contact with Robert and Mitch as I shook the dice in my hand, the look on their faces was priceless.

Seconds later, I strutted with my Detroit Swag into the middle of the living room, got down on one knee, and rubbed the dice in my hands before throwing them in the air with one hand, and catching them with the other. Then, I turned in the opposite direction, blindly threw the dice on the ground behind me with confidence, and stood back up before strutting away and throwing my arms up in victory because I just knew I had rolled a four, five, six and won the game. That is, until Mitch, Robert, and everyone else in the room busted out laughing.

"Mark, man, you suck!" Robert teased, laughing himself to tears.

"You rolled a one, two three, bro'!" Mitch exclaimed, doubled over with laughter. "You didn't win shit!"

For the next two and a half hours, everyone in the living room had a great time jamming to music, playing gender reveal games, eating finger foods and cake, and cracking jokes on each other. Then, Trisha handed me an envelope and gave me the honor of opening it, silently reading the card inside, and busting one of the gold balloons in the middle of the room to reveal the baby's gender.

After reading the card, I had a smile on my face a mile wide as I walked over with a needle in my hand and popped the gold balloon containing the blue confetti. The room erupted with claps, cheers, and congratulations for Robert, Trisha, and their baby boy and I couldn't have been happier for my bro.

Afterwards, Trisha put the music back on and everyone started partying and having a good time again. Rosh and the other women were as giddy as high school girls in the dining room, and Robert, Mitch, myself, and a few other men were gathered around the coffee table in the living room playing spades. But even though I was partying and having a good time, I couldn't shake the feeling in my gut telling me that my mom was dead. At the same time, though, I couldn't ignore the hope I had that she was alive. After all, almost seven hours had passed since the shooting at Tops, and I had not received a single call from the hospital, police, or sheriff which I took as a good sign.

But at 9:03 p.m., my cell phone began to ring and for the first time since the shooting, the caller wasn't someone in my family. "Mark," Rosh yelled over the music as she walked towards me. "It's a private number."

At that moment, my heart sank into my stomach, and I knew that I was minutes away from receiving news that would make me extremely happy or tear my world apart. If only I had known that the news I was about to receive would confirm my worst fear.

CHAPTER 7
Suicidal Thoughts – Notorious B.I.G

osh approached me with my ringing cell phone in her hand and everything around me seemed to slow to a crawl. At that moment, I wondered if the emotions deep inside me would bubble to the surface and burst through like a volcanic eruption if I received traumatic news about my mom.

Seconds later, Rosh's mom shuffled us into the bathroom to have some privacy and closed the door behind her as she left. Then, Rosh answered the call. "Hello?" she asked with a shaky voice.

"This is Officer Rhodes with the Buffalo Police Department. May I speak with Mark Talley, please."

"This is his wife. He's right here with me."

"Mr. Talley, please acknowledge your presence on this call."

"I'm here," I said through the lump in my throat.

"Mr. Talley, I'm sorry to inform you that your mother, Geraldine Talley, was one of the victims killed in the attack at Tops today."

Rosh immediately began to cry uncontrollably as she mourned the death of my mom. And me? I sat there waiting for the eruption of my emotions to start. But there was nothing. No emotions bubbling to the surface. No emotional eruption. I wanted to cry. I really did. But I couldn't. I just couldn't cry. I don't know why I couldn't. My body felt numb. I just felt as if I was frozen. I didn't know what to do, how to feel, or what to say after receiving the worst news of my life.

"Mr. Talley, are you still there?" Officer Rhodes asked.

"Yeah," I muttered as Rosh wailed with tears cascading down both cheeks.

"Do you have any questions I can answer for you at this time?" Officer Rhodes asked.

"No."

After hanging up, I held Rosh tight and kissed her on the forehead. She was still crying, and I was still frozen. *It's going to be a long next few months*, I thought to myself.

After a few minutes passed, Rosh and I exited the bathroom and returned to the living room where Rosh's mom, her sister, and several other women were crying. Suddenly, everyone crowded around me and started hugging me, touching me, and saying how sorry they were as Rosh continued to cry. At that moment, I knew that I was going to be dealing with this type of B.S. for months to come. So, I resorted to dark humor and started joking with Rosh as she cried because, like I said, laughter is a great coping mechanism and I desperately needed something to help me cope with the darkness I was experiencing.

"What are you crying this much for?" I asked in my usual sarcastic way. "You would think she's your mother."

Once again, Rosh didn't find my comments funny, she just continued to sob.

We stayed at Robert and Trisha's apartment for one more hour, but, as you can imagine, no one was in the mood to celebrate after finding out that my mom was killed. And on the drive back home, I still didn't know how to react to my mom's death. So, I did what I do best. I looked at Rosh and figured I try to make a joke. I always said if you can make a woman laugh, you can get anything from her. "I bet she didn't have her cane when she died," I said. "If she did, I don't know why she didn't use it to hit the bullets."

Rosh didn't say a word. She just stared out the windshield like she was in some sort of trance. I knew Rosh better than anyone and knew the reason she wasn't talking was not because of me. It was because she was in shock and disbelief. So, I continued. "If her knees and hips were in good shape, she could've ducked, dodged, and ran from the bullets."

Rosh continued to drive silently.

Eventually, I got tired of talking to myself, so I quietly sat in the passenger's seat and thought about my mom. My mom and I joked with each other constantly. Her jokes were more lighthearted and mine were darker. She wasn't always a fan of my dark humor, but those funny moments when she would laugh at one of my jokes were among the best. And no matter what your opinion is of the jokes I just mentioned, I'm willing to bet all my worldly possessions that my mom was laughing when I said she was ducking and dodging the bullets.

It was about 10:30 p.m. and Rosh was emotionally drained. So, she immediately brushed her teeth, put on her pajamas, and climbed into bed while I took Porkchop outside to use the bathroom. And after taking a hot shower to calm my nerves, I laid down next to Rosh. She was already sleeping, and I was hoping to go to sleep, too. But I couldn't and ended up staring at the ceiling as the roller coaster inside my stomach moved up the invisible track again, gained momentum inside me until it reached the highest point, and plunged into darkness, terrifying me on the inside repeatedly until finally, I fell asleep and started to dream.

I dreamed that I was standing in the middle of a wheat field. I looked all around me trying to figure out where I was and that's when I saw my mom in the distance. She was at a train station and was smiling and waving to me as she prepared to board a train.

I must admit, my first thought when I saw her was, '*Why a train? Why not a plane or an automobile?*' Suddenly, it hit me that she wasn't waving hello—she was waving goodbye. I didn't want her to go so I ran as fast as I could to stop her from boarding. But I was running against the wind and couldn't get there fast enough. And when I saw a plume of steam rise from the train after she disappeared inside, I fell on my knees and cried as I watched the train pull away and chug out of sight.

The pain I felt in my dream jolted me awake. *What the hell is wrong with me?* I screamed in my head. *I love you, mom! Why can't I cry? Why can't I feel anything?*

I tossed and turned all night as I tried to return to sleep. But the roller coaster inside my stomach wouldn't let me. I wanted to know a little more about what happened to my mom, so I scrolled through the news clippings on my phone app. And when I discovered that my mom's killer was an eighteen-year-old White boy, I quickly closed the news app and began tormenting myself with all the 'why' questions.

Why wasn't I more vocal in expressing my love for my mom? She was such a loving woman who told me that she loved me almost every time we talked or saw each other. And she definitely knew that I loved her. But why wasn't I capable of understanding how much it would've meant to her to hear those three little words from her only son? I mean—I've always been a low emotions person, so I rarely said it back to her when she said it to me.

Why didn't I call my mom a week ago to wish her Happy Mother's Day instead of sending her a text message from Rosh's phone? I mean—I didn't even tell her the text message was from me. I just assumed she knew. Why couldn't I see how impersonal sending a text message was and just called her from Rosh's phone so she could hear my voice? At least I would've known that she knew it was me, her double scoop of dark chocolate, who wished her Happy Mother's Day.

The final question, the question I asked myself then and still do now…. *Why did I take for granted how long I would have her in my life?* If I had known this is how my life with her was going to end, I would have hugged my mom so tight the last time I saw her and never let go.

After beating myself up thinking about all the things I should've, would've, could've done, I finally fell asleep around 4 a.m.

On the morning of May 15th, I awoke to the sound of Rosh weeping next to me. I wanted to take her into my arms and comfort her, but I couldn't muster enough strength to move. So, I just laid there, staring at the ceiling, and grieving on the inside as Porkchop whined in the hallway. I laid there because I just didn't know what to do. I was afraid to go outside because I knew that if I saw anyone who resembled my mom's killer—you know, someone who looked like the stereotypical White country boy with a porn 'stache and beard stubble, I might snap and immediately try to hurt that person. And my head was so messed up in that moment. Like I said earlier, if I had known on the morning of May 14th that by 2:28 p.m. my mother would be dead, I would've waited for her killer at the store and showed him the true meaning of the word 'pain'.

At this point, I still wasn't mentally ready to hear specific details about what happened at Tops and thought avoiding news coverage would be easy because I'd never been the type to watch the news on TV or listen to it on the radio. But when I scrolled through the news on my phone, the shooting at Tops seemed to be the only thing I kept seeing. I was already feeling some kind of way after losing my mom and constantly seeing the news clips in my newsfeed didn't help.

After finally getting out of bed, I stumbled around in a fog—you know, just going through the motions of my daily routine and trying to stay busy to keep from thinking about my mom's last moments and the terror she must've felt. And after calling into work to request bereavement leave that morning, I sat on the couch with Rosh and just played video games all day. Neither one of us had much of an appetite, so we didn't eat much, just snacked on little things throughout the day.

For the next one to two days, I followed the same routine: I got up without brushing my teeth or showering, and just spent the day playing video games. I didn't want to talk to anyone or see anyone—I just wanted to be left alone, as I didn't know how to deal with the situation. I wanted to cry but couldn't seem to express my emotions. My feelings of depression were compounded by my desires for self-harm, which only made me feel worse.

I am aware that I am different and that the things that make me angry or upset me may be different from those of other people. I even recognize that the things that make me angry or frustrate me can seem silly or irrational. For example, during this period, I became very frustrated with the large amount of food that was being sent to my place by people who cared. It made me so angry because the food I was receiving was not the type of food I normally eat; it was all Italian food. If it had been pizza, I would have been thrilled, but it was nothing but pastas, lasagnas, and fettuccine alfredos and I just couldn't take it. Now, Rosh loved eating Italian food and each time she opened the hot meal containers we received, it made me happy to see a smile on her face. Don't get me wrong though, I was grateful to the organizations who sent us the food, it just so happened that Italian food was my least favorite cuisine.

During the first few days after May 14th, almost every dream I had, my mom was in it. It was like clockwork, and I began looking forward to my dreams. On May 15th, I took a nap in the middle of the day and had a dream that was on the funnier side.

I dreamed that my mom and I were at a comedy club, and each comedian that came up would throw food at the audience. However, when the last comedian of the day stepped on stage, before he could even deliver a joke, we began flinging food at him. Unsurprisingly, he didn't appreciate it and began chasing us around the club. With both of us exhausted, we ended up taking a break in the same spot. As I looked over at my mom, I noticed that she was crying and asked her why. She sadly explained that she had run out of food to throw.

But later that night, as I got deeper into my sleep, my dream was more emotional.

I dreamed that my mom was standing in a lush green meadow and wearing a yellow gown that shimmered like the sun against her cocoa complexion. I must have been about ten years old in my dream and remembered how beautiful she looked as her microbraids and dress blew in the gentle breeze. "There's my double scoop of dark chocolate," she said, reaching her arms out to me and smiling.

Words cannot describe the joy I felt when I ran into her opened arms and hugged her tight—or the heartbreak I felt on the morning of May 16th when my ringing cell phone jolted me awake and I realized that my mom was still gone.

"Sev- 7 a.m.?" I stuttered, glancing at the clock on the nightstand. "Who the hell calls at this hour?"

"Who is it?" Rosh muttered before quickly falling back asleep.

As I laid in bed listening to the phone ring, my head was spinning as I thought about how much my life had changed during the last 48 hours. If only I had known that my life was about to change even more.

CHAPTER 8

Interlude – J. Cole

I was tired, angry, and not in the mood for conversation so I ignored the ringing phone. Suddenly, I realized that I forgot to put my phone back on do not disturb. What if Officer Rhodes was calling with more information about my mom?

I slowly sat up and grabbed my cell phone from the nightstand. When I answered it and was greeted by a reporter who said she got my phone number from the Office of Victim Services, I had a feeling that her call was the first of what would become many calls about the death of my mom.

Immediately after hanging up with the first reporter, my phone rang again and it kept ringing all day long as I received call after call from family members and well-wishers expressing their condolences, as well as reporters and journalists at the local and national level wanting to talk to me about my mom. And every time the phone rang, the introvert in me felt like throwing it into Lake Erie and running away from the chaos. But instead of sulking or wanting to run away, I took the advice I always gave my mom when times were tough. I manned up and did my best to honor her as I answered each call and responded to each question.

But it was the last call that I received from a reporter at about 5 p.m. that caused tremors of anger, hurt, and flat-out fury to churn deep inside me. You see, it was during this call that I discovered that the mass shooting at Tops had been classified as a racially motivated terrorist attack; that the killer was a racist who livestreamed his killing spree on social media for other racists to see; that he targeted the eastside of Buffalo because of its large population of Black people; and that he drove two hundred miles and previously visited Tops to scope it out before returning to murder as many Black people as he could.

The rage I felt burning deep inside me as the reporter continued to speak was like death by a thousand cuts but to the umpteenth degree. It's one thing to think that this White person killed your mom because they were randomly looking for people to shoot that day, but it's an entirely different thing to realize that your mom was targeted and murdered by a racist, armed with a semi-automatic rifle and body armor, because he wanted to hunt down and kill Black people, including my mom who had nothing to defend herself except lunch meat!

Adding to my outrage was the fact that, once again, another White racist killer was calmly taken into custody by police alive and well after killing ten Black people in our community. Now, you and I both know that if the situation were reversed and it was a Black man shooting up a grocery store full of White people, he would've been killed on sight, no questions asked. But like I said, I guess I can find solace in the fact that they didn't take him to Burger King afterwards.

After hanging up the phone, I was filled with so much rage and felt like I was going to explode from the inside out and cry for the first time since my mom was killed. And, I'll be honest, I was looking forward to crying because I wanted some proof for myself that I am not this cold. I wanted some physical proof that I loved my mother because it seemed that everyone was crying except me and that was destroying me inside.

A knock on the door distracted me and caused my inner emotions to return to the deep. "I'll get it," I said, rubbing my hands together and licking my lips. "Maybe someone sent some wings or sesame chicken this time."

Rosh walked over to the door just as I opened it—and there it was. Two more bags from the same Italian restaurant that brought us food yesterday.

I stood in the doorway frozen just blinking as I stared at the bags on the floor. Then, Rosh picked them up and put them on the kitchen table. *I may kill myself if I have to keep eating Italian food*, I thought as I closed the front door.

The food was another gift from the same local organization that sent us food the day before. And when Rosh opened the containers of food, revealing chicken alfredo and more garlic bread, she was smiling from ear to ear as she made her plate and dug in. And me? I ordered McDonald's from Door Dash and devoured it.

After eating, Rosh and I sat on the couch in the living room. I was still deeply troubled by the phone call with the last reporter and I'm sure that had something to do with my negative attitude. "I don't understand why people send food when tragedy strikes," I said.

"I think it's a tradition for some people— a way for them to let you know they're thinking about you while you're grieving."

"I get that, but why send pasta and bread? Isn't there a tradition that says when someone dies, send pies or cakes or pizza or wings? Or a tradition that says just send money so they can buy food they actually want to eat? If it's not a tradition it should be. Who do I call to get this going?"

After cuddling on the couch with Rosh for a while as we attempted to watch a movie, and getting Porkchop into her crate, we turned in for the night. But even though I didn't have a hard time falling to sleep, it was hell trying to stay asleep because of the new information I found out about my mom's killer that weighed heavily on my mind. It was kind of like trying to sleep with heartburn or acid reflux and having the nasty taste of racist asshole constantly shooting up my esophagus.

On the morning of May 17th, I woke up groggy and disappointed on the inside because I didn't see my mom in my dreams last night. I missed her and found myself becoming addicted to my dreams and wanting to sleep more than I wanted to be awake. So, I just laid in bed, unable to motivate myself to do anything other than going back to sleep in hopes that I would see my mom.

Hours later, I was still trying to return to sleep. By this time, Rosh was awake and had taken Porkchop outside to use the bathroom. I didn't know what time it was but assumed it was around 10 a.m. Since I couldn't sleep, I sat on the side of the bed and really didn't know what to do because I wasn't ready to engage with anyone outside of our apartment.

Then, I heard the front door open. Second later, Porkchop came barreling into my bedroom before leaping on the bed and showing me slobbery love. And after giving her a few minutes of much needed attention, I put on my sweatpants and went to the bathroom to relieve myself as Rosh called out to me. "Mark, are you hungry?"

"A little bit," I replied before flushing the toilet.

I washed my hands as the cell phone on my nightstand began to ring. I quickly returned to the bedroom and answered the first call in what became a series of calls from various family members and friends. Some called to tell me that President Biden was going to be at Tops that afternoon; some called to ask if I wanted to meet the President; some called to talk about the possibility of suing Tops, the city of Buffalo, or the gun manufacturers.

I held the phone in my hand during the last call, but my brain was in overload as I tried to insulate myself from the nightmare that had become my life—I mean, a racist asshole brutally killed my mom three days ago, and all these people were calling me about things I couldn't have cared less about in that moment because none of it would bring my mom back. I was drowning on the inside and even considered checking myself into CPEP which, as you may recall, provided emergency psychiatric services at the hospital where I worked, but I decided not to because I still wasn't ready to face the outside world. So, after telling Rosh about all the nonsense these people had called me about, I did the next best thing, I detached from my reality.

First, I changed the location on my phone's news app from Buffalo to Detroit to block out daily updates about the shooting at Tops. Next, I blocked almost everyone that called me that day on my phone so they couldn't call me anymore and even blocked other family members and friends who had not called me yet just in case they tried. Finally, I popped three melatonin gummies in my mouth to block my ability to stay awake so that I could return to the serenity of sleep, dreams, and, most importantly, my mom.

After taking the melatonin, I went to the bathroom and relieved myself one more time. Then, I returned to the bedroom, climbed back into bed, and ate the bacon, scrambled eggs, and toast that Rosh put on my nightstand. And after taking a few gulps of orange juice, I laid down on the pillow and focused on my mom as my eyes became heavy. The next thing I knew, I had drifted off to sleep and into a dream.

I dreamed I was frantically walking around a big city carrying a wallet size picture of my mom. I didn't know the name of the city I was in, only that it was crowded with hundreds, if not thousands, of senior citizens enjoying everything the city had to offer from concerts in the park to art festivals in the street. I felt out of place as the only thirty-something man in a sea of senior citizens but was hopeful that someone had seen my mom.

After showing her picture to hundreds of seniors and getting nowhere, I sat down on a nearby park bench and closed my eyes to think.

"You can't sleep here, fella!" a silver-haired man said, poking my leg with his cane.

"I wasn't sleeping, I was thinking about my mom."

"Oh yeah? Where is she?"

"I don't know. I can't find her."

"You can't? Well, sitting here on your laurels ain't gonna help! When you gonna get your head out of your ass and man up?"

What the 'F'? I angrily thought to myself. "Old man, you don't want none of this, I'll—"

My thoughts were interrupted by an elderly couple talking shit within earshot of me.

"I told you he wouldn't man up," the old geezer said.

"When you're right, you're right," the woman replied, shaking her head. "He's not a double scoop of dark chocolate. He's a triple scoop of cow manure."

I was so annoyed and consumed by my thoughts that I didn't realize someone had sat down on the bench next to me. When I turned to see who it was, I froze. It was my mom, completely covered in blood and staring at me. She was breathing heavily and appeared to be extremely angry. "Maaark!" she screamed in a horrifying deep voice as blood poured from her mouth. "There's my double scoop of dark chocolate!"

Suddenly, she grabbed my wrist with her bloody hand, and I let out a blood curdling scream. *"Rooooosh!"*

The next thing I knew, Rosh was shaking me by the shoulders. "Mark!" she yelled as she continued to shake me. "Mark! Wake up!"

I woke up trembling and covered in sweat. "Rosh," I drowsily said.

"You were screaming in your sleep! I ran in here as fast as I could."

After telling Rosh about my horrific nightmare, I knew that I couldn't let another day go by without hearing the truth about what happened to my mom from the only person who was with her—Malcolm, her fiancé. And as I mentally prepared myself to go see him, I knew it would be hard. This would be the first time that I went to their home since my mom died.

I climbed out of bed and quickly got dressed. A few minutes later, Rosh and I were on our way to my mother's house for the first time since she was killed.

I had a great relationship with Malcolm as I mentioned previously and called ahead of time to see if it would be alright for us to stop by. I wanted to discuss what happened with my mother on May 14th, but also wanted to make sure he was doing alright, both mentally and physically.

We arrived at my mom's house around 6 p.m. and when I saw Malcolm's car in the driveway, a lump formed in my throat—I didn't know if I was ready to finally face my fears. And as Rosh parked the car in the driveway behind his, I took a deep breath in and released it quickly.

"Are you okay, Mark?" she asked.

"I think so. But Rosh, I think I need to do this alone."

"I understand," she said with compassion. "I'll be right here waiting for you."

I leaned over and gave Rosh a long and gentle kiss on the lips. Then, I exited the car and began walking up the sidewalk. Suddenly, the front door opened, and Malcolm was standing in the doorway. "It's good to see you, Mark," he said.

"It's good to see you, too." I walked up and gave him a hug.

Malcolm was in his sixties and, like I said, was a low emotions guy like me. And even though my mom was the love of his life, he wasn't overly emotional about her murder—at least not on the outside. But I'm sure he probably felt horrible about it on the inside because they had been together for the last seven years.

After waving to Rosh in the car, he turned around and walked into the house with me following close behind. But as soon as I entered the doorway, the sweet scent of my mom hit me like a punch to the gut and I wasn't sure if I was mentally and emotionally ready to hear the details about what happened to my mom. Looking back on it now, I can definitely tell you I was not.

CHAPTER 9
Novacane – Frank Ocean

Malcolm sat in my mom's favorite chair as I made my way to the couch and sat down. "I'm sorry I didn't come by sooner to check on you," I said.

"No need to be sorry," he replied. "I understand. I know you needed time."

"Is there anything you need?" I asked. "I mean, are you alright? Are you okay?"

"I'm doing okay, some days are better than others. Do you need anything?"

"Yes, I want to know what happened at Tops."

I was feeling tense and leaned back on the couch to relax. Then, I closed my eyes to paint a picture in my mind as he began to explain what happened on May 14th.

"Gerri and I went to Foot of Ferry together around eleven-fifteen that morning," he said. "We stayed there almost three hours just enjoying quality time together laughing, talking, loving on each other, stuff like that."

When Malcolm said they went to Foot of Ferry, I smiled on the inside because I knew they had a good time. He took my mom there every week when the weather was warm, and it was one of her favorite places to go.

"We were on our way home," Malcolm continued, "when Gerri said she needed to pick up a few items to make some food for tonight and tomorrow, so we went to Tops."

"We went inside and walked past the cash registers," he continued. "She didn't need much, just some bologna and cheese, but then Gerri remembered that she needed some iced tea, so we split up. I went to the aisle where the iced tea was, and she took the buggy and went to a different aisle to get the bologna and cheese."

"After grabbing the tea from the shelf," he continued. "I walked around the corner to return to her, but that's when the killer came into the store and started shooting people at the front. I froze and then I saw the security guard and the killer shooting back and forth at each other as everyone started running to the back of the store screaming. But then the killer saw me and started shooting at me, so I started ducking and dodging bullets that were flying by my head while yelling for Gerri."

As Malcolm described what happened, I was trembling on the inside thinking about the terror my mom must've felt as she stood in the aisle of the grocery store and heard the gunshots and people screaming.

"I knew I couldn't outrun him—he's a young man and I'm not," he continued. "So, I turned the corner and squeezed myself inside of the cooler where they keep all the frozen stuff—the ice cream, frozen foods—stuff like that. I was in there for a few minutes and then I saw him searching for me. I thought he saw me, and I was about to die. But he didn't and after a few minutes of walking back and forth trying to find me, he left."

The room went quiet. I was still trembling on the inside and opened my eyes. "Did you get hurt squeezing into the cooler?" I asked.

"No, just some bruises," he replied, showing me the bruises on his forearms.

"Did you try to find my mom after you came out?" I asked.

"I wanted to, but the police were there, and they wouldn't let me."

Hearing the details about what happened to my mom on May 14th was more difficult than I thought it would be. And yet, I still didn't shed a single tear which made no sense to me even as an introvert with low emotions.

After thanking Malcolm for sharing my mom's final moments and giving him a hug, he said, "Gerri always said that if anything should ever happen to her, to tell you that you have the first opportunity to go through her items and take anything of sentimental value."

Then, Malcolm left to give me some privacy.

I stood up and slowly walked from room to room collecting things that belonged to my mom including a couple of dessert plates she often used, the robe she regularly wore, a bunch of other hard to describe items, and her favorite blouse.

My mom was big on taking pictures and had accumulated a bunch of photo albums over the years to hold her precious memories. I wanted to take them with me, so I headed to the little computer room where she spent most of her time. But when I opened the door, her sweet scent was especially strong and overwhelmed my senses. And as I stood in the doorway staring at the empty room and thinking of everything we'd been through, it hit me like a sledgehammer to the chest—my mom was gone, and I'd never see her, kiss her, or hug her again.

Before I knew it, my heart was racing a million miles a minute as my chest began to tighten, and I struggled to breathe. "Mom!" I cried out, holding on for dear life to her robe, blouse, and dishes.

And as salty tears formed and clouded my vision, I began to cry for the first time since the day my mom was killed. I cried uncontrollably, hysterically, and convulsively. I could barely breathe and couldn't wipe away the tears fast enough.

My body shook uncontrollably as I stood in the doorway with snot running from my nose and a river of tears streaming down my cheeks.

Suddenly, I dropped the items in my hands and stormed into the bathroom across the hall. "Momma, don't go!" I screamed, punching the wall harder and harder until my knuckles bled and the pain in my hands was greater than the pain in my heart. I was falling apart at the seams, hyperventilating, and wailing as loud as I could before my legs gave out and I fell to the ground.

My breathing was labored, and my body felt weak, but I managed to slide my swollen hand into my pants pocket to get my cell phone and call Rosh. "Rosh can you come inside please—"

Before I could finish my sentence, I heard Rosh running down the hallway. Seconds later, she fell to the floor in the bathroom and held me in her warm embrace. I buried my face in her chest and continued to cry. "It's okay, baby," she said, rocking me back and forth and kissing my forehead repeatedly. And when I raised my head up and her eyes met mine, I saw that she was crying, too.

Although I was overwhelmed by grief and experiencing pain unlike anything I'd ever felt, a part of me was glad that I finally cried, and that Rosh was able to see on the outside what I've been feeling on the inside this whole time.

After I regained my composure, Rosh and I left the bathroom, picked up the things I dropped on the ground, and grabbed the picture albums from my mom's desk. As we drove home, I shared the details that Malcolm shared with me about what happened to my mom, and she cried the whole way home.

"Did it help you to hear those details?" she asked as we pulled into our apartment complex.

"A little bit, but he didn't know what happened to my mom after they were separated because he didn't see. He was hiding. And when he came out, the police wouldn't let him look for her."

"I'm sorry, baby. I know you need closure."

"One of the reporters that called me said the killer was wearing a camera on his helmet and livestreamed his killing spree on social media. She said thirteen people were shot and ten of them died. Tomorrow, I'm going to try to find the video. I need to see my mom."

After we made it into our apartment, I put the picture albums on the coffee table in the living room. Neither one of us had much of an appetite so we took Porkchop outside for a walk and to use the bathroom. When we returned, Rosh made a couple of peanut butter and jelly sandwiches and after we ate, we turned in for the night with Porkchop laying at the foot of the bed.

On the morning of May 18th, I climbed out of bed as Rosh continued to sleep. Porkchop leaped out of bed, ran to the front door, and whined as I quickly put on my sweatpants and shoes.

After taking Porkchop outside to use the bathroom, I returned to my apartment. Porkchop went to her food bowl in the kitchen, and I went to the living room, sat down on the couch, and used my phone to search online for the video. A few minutes later, I found the video and stared at it for a few seconds. Then, I braced myself and pushed the play button.

Suddenly, I was looking at the killer in the rearview mirror as he drove in the Tops parking lot. He had a strip of dark paint across his nose and was wearing some kind of head covering. "This ends right here," he said out loud. "I'm going in."

I caught a glimpse of the beige gloves he wore as he turned the steering wheel to the right, and the rifle that was propped up against the passenger seat. And as he drove towards the main entrance, I immediately noticed four Black people in front of the store: a man standing behind a car with an open trunk, a woman walking towards the killer in the parking lot, another woman standing in front of the entrance with a grocery cart, and another man standing next to her. And as they went about their day, completely unaware of the racist killer in their midst, my body tensed up again.

I quickly paused the video. "I can't do this," I said, shaking my head rapidly. "She watched me take my first breath. Can I seriously watch her take her last?"

I sat there, staring at my phone, and wondering what would be worse, knowing the full truth about what happened to my mom on May 14th or not knowing. After going back and forth, I decided that not knowing would be worse and pushed the play button.

The video resumed with the car pulling up and stopping in front of the store's entrance. I felt sick to my stomach as I watched the killer put the car in park, open the door, and get out with the rifle in both hands, quickly cocking it. Then, without any warning, he opened fire. In less than two seconds, he shot the woman walking in the parking lot in the head twice and the man behind his trunk once. The woman walking fell on the pavement face first as the man, who was still alive, fell and landed on his back behind the car.

Seconds later, the killer slightly turned to the left and sprayed six bullets into the woman standing in front of the entrance with the grocery cart and the man standing next to her as a fifth person casually walked out of the store, realized what was happening, and quickly ran back in. The woman fell face first to the ground, knocking over the grocery cart, at the same time as the man fell and landed on his side. Within a second, the killer turned his attention back to the man lying on his back behind the car and fired three more shots into him.

The killer was void of all human emotions and didn't care about the lives he was taking or the families he was destroying. I was trembling as I watched the events unfold in what seemed more like a horrific first-person shooter videogame than a gruesome reality.

Seconds later, he randomly shot five bullets through the store window. I bawled my fists as he made his way to the entrance and brutally shot the woman with the grocery cart two more times in the head.

I was stunned. In less than seven seconds, four Black people who were alive and well were now lying motionless on the hot pavement and I knew some, if not all of them, were dead. And I'll be honest, I hated that racist P.O.S with every fiber of my being and wanted to hurt him so bad. And as I thought about the total number of people the reporter said were shot, my jaw clenched. There were nine people remaining to be shot—and one of them was my mom.

I heard screaming in the distance as the killer entered the store and aimed his rifle to the right. I sighed in relief when I didn't see anyone there. But when he turned to the left, I swallowed hard, realizing that my relief was short-lived when I saw two Black women just a few feet away as other people who were further away ran. Both had been hit by the bullets he shot through the window before he entered the store, and both were still alive.

I got choked up as one woman wearing a long summer skirt slowly crawled on her hands and knees trying to get to safety. Both of her sandals had fallen off and were scattered behind her and I could tell that she was in excruciating pain. The other woman was lying on her side writhing in agony near the potato chip shelves. As soon as he saw them, he opened fire shooting the crawling woman in her thighs four more times until she collapsed and the other woman two more times in her back. I watched in horror, unable to comprehend the evil that came to Buffalo that day.

The video became distorted as the killer opened fire on people further away in the row in front of the cash registers. I couldn't tell how many shots were fired or how many people were there, but I hoped he was moving on. I hoped he had forgotten about the second woman lying on her back and that she might've been one of the people who were shot but survived.

My hopes were instantly dashed, though, when he turned his head to the right and refocused his attention on her. She had rolled onto her back while he was shooting at the others and was holding her stomach with both hands while moaning in agonizing pain. I'll be honest, I was angry, I wanted to shove that rifle so far up his ass that he'd shit bullets for a month.

The video buffered as he walked past her and stood behind her head. She continued to moan as he reloaded his rifle and I saw the words "Monkey" and "Nigger" painted or scratched on the rifle's surface, along with other illegible words. Suddenly, he cocked his rifle and mercilessly shot her in the head twice before stepping over her body as the distorted video became clear and turning the corner to the right.

I quickly paused the video. My whole body was trembling as I realized that the killer was intentionally trying to shoot every Black person he saw in the head to guarantee death. At that moment, I felt sick to my stomach because I knew I would eventually see my mother hunted down and shot like an animal.

CHAPTER 10
Day 'N' Nite – Kid Cudi

After realizing that the killer was intentionally shooting Black people in the head, I was extremely upset. I stood up and started pacing back and forth across the living room. "No," I muttered to myself, shaking my head rapidly. "No, absolutely not."

As I continued pacing, I was torn. Part of me wanted to stop the video and create my own version of how my mom was killed, a version that although tragic would be less brutal—less cruel. But the other part of me knew that I had to face my fears no matter how horrifying they were. Face the reality of what happened to my mom and not some sugar-coated version if I was ever going to be able to move forward.

I was breathing heavily as I sat back down on the couch and pressed the play button on the video. The next thing I knew, the killer was exchanging gunfire with a Black man who I now recognized as the security guard in the row in front of the cash registers. When I saw this,

I immediately thought of Malcolm, my mom's fiancé, who said that after he got the iced tea, he turned the corner to return to my mom and saw the killer and the security guard exchanging gunfire.

The video became distorted again and I couldn't tell what was going on. When it cleared, I no longer saw the security guard and instinctively knew that he had been shot. But when the killer began heading his way, a chill went down my spine because I knew what he was planning to do next. I knew he was planning to shoot him in the head because injuring him wasn't enough. He wanted to kill him like he did with the others. As he walked in the direction of the security guard, the quality of the video cleared up and I saw someone else who had been shot to the left of the killer. It was a White woman who was standing in the small area in between the men and women bathrooms. I didn't know if she was hiding there and had been shot, or if she walked out of the bathroom and had been shot in the crossfire, but as he walked towards the security guard, she fell forward directly in front of him, and he paid her no attention. He had no desire to verify that she was dead or shoot her in the head to guarantee that she was dead and that just reinforced what I already knew. He wasn't there to shoot White people; he was there to specifically hunt and kill Black people.

Immediately after the White woman to the left of the killer fell to the ground, he realized that someone else was on the ground in the checkout lane to the right of him. The person was a White man and appeared to have been shot as well. And although I couldn't see the killer's face, he seemed to be in some kind of trance, and I could literally feel his excitement as he quickly aimed the rifle to kill the person on the ground that he obviously thought was Black. "Noooo!" the man screamed, raising his hand in defense.

His scream appeared to snap the killer out of his trance and made him realize that he was about to kill a White man. "Sorry," he said to the man on the ground.

Then, something seemed to distract him from continuing to pursue the security guard because he quickly turned around and headed through the checkout area. The video became distorted again so I couldn't see what he saw, but I remembered Malcolm's chilling words. He said that he saw the killer and the security guard exchanging gunfire and then the killer saw him and started shooting at him as he ran and ducked and dodge bullets.

I was honestly incensed when the perpetrator apologized to the White man he was about to shoot. It just felt like a cruel act of even more racism. Not only had he come to this Black community to take innocent Black lives, but he also showed remorse for a White person caught in the crossfire and that felt like a double insult and was a painful blow to my soul. And even though the words on his rifle clearly showed who he was hunting with the intention to kill, by sparing this White man's life he proved that even in the face of death when things are supposed to be equal, there was racism on top of racism and White lives still carried a greater value.

I paused the video again. The reporter I spoke with on the phone told me that thirteen people were shot on May 14th and I had seen numerous shootings but had yet to see my mom. I sat back on the couch and recalled the number of people I had seen shot. "Let's see," I whispered, closing my eyes to count. "Four people outside, two women by the entrance, the security guard, and two White people. That's nine."

A lump immediately formed in my throat as realization set in that somewhere among the last four people that would be shot that day was my mom and seeing her in this video would be the last time I'd ever see her alive.

I was feeling anxious and sat up straight on the couch. Then, I took a deep breath, exhaled quickly, and pushed the play button once more. The video resumed with the killer spraying bullets randomly which, I believed, were intended to shoot Malcolm, but as he briskly walked forward, he found a Black man hiding in the checkout lane and shot him in the back of the head. *That's ten*, I thought to myself, as my body trembled with anger and fear.

By this point, my stomach was in knots. There were three people remaining to be shot and I wondered if my mom would be the next person the killer saw as he began briskly walking from aisle to aisle. Sadly, a few seconds later, he found a Black man standing in an aisle and appeared to shoot him multiple times in the head. "Eleven," I whispered to myself as he began to fall over, and the killer immediately started walking the aisles again.

My heart was pounding so hard it hurt as I assumed that my mom was next. I paused the video again and started rocking back and forth as my anxiety reached an all-time high and I tried to cope. I closed my eyes, took a deep breath in, and slowly released it seconds later as I stopped rocking and pushed the play button again.

Mere seconds later, the killer found a Black woman standing in another aisle and shot her in the head multiple times as well. And as she began falling to the ground, he started walking away.

I quickly paused the video and immediately broke out in a cold sweat. *Mo-Mom was the last person killed?* I thought to myself as a bead of sweat dripped from my brow. *His rampage came to an end after he killed my mom?*

I sat on the couch as still as a statue knowing that the next Black person the killer was going to find was my mom. And although I knew she was going to be killed, I couldn't bear the thought of her being shot in the head as so many beloved people before her had been.

I can't adequately describe the feeling that came over me when I realized I was seconds away from seeing my mom. I can say that I was extremely overwhelmed, but that is a severe understatement. I can say that I felt a deep mix of fear and sadness, knowing that my mom was in mortal danger and there was nothing I could do to protect her. I can say that I felt helpless knowing that her safety, her well-being, her very life was in the hands of a killer who was filled with hatred and prejudice against her because she was Black.

I was terrified and shaking all over as I tried to find the strength I needed to press the play button and see my mom alive for the very last time. I'll be honest, the decision to press the play button at this moment was one of the hardest decisions I've ever had to make because I knew that that the only reason I had this opportunity was because the killer had her in his sights and I was seeing her through his camera. And although I knew that my mom was about to be killed, I still couldn't stomach the thought of her being shot in the head. I just couldn't handle her dying in such a brutal way. None of the ten Black people there deserved to die in such a brutal way.

But as hard as the decision was to make, I also knew that I couldn't walk away. I couldn't let the video end there. The thing that hurts the most is that the only video that I had of my mother was the one of her being killed in cold blood. I had no other videos of her, only countless pictures, memories, messages, and other mementos. This video was the only video, to my knowledge, that showed her still alive, so I knew I had to watch the rest because I desperately needed to see my mom alive even though I'd have to live with the fact that it was also the video that showed her dying.

Giant tears clouded my eyes as I reluctantly pushed the play button. The video resumed with the killer walking several more aisles down and finding my mom. She was wearing leggings with a long blouse and was standing next to her grocery cart in the middle of the aisle.

I quickly paused the video again. *Come on man, not like this,* I said to myself, gently running my finger along her image, trying to memorize every line and every curve. *I can't see my mom die like this.*

After a few minutes, I reluctantly pushed the play button again as tears dropped onto my phone. A split second later, I watched as the killer shot my mom in the head twice. It happened so fast—she didn't even have time to react. And as she began to fall forward face first with no one there to catch her or break her fall, the killer walked away, and I lost sight of her before she hit the ground. Second later, the video abruptly ended.

The entire video was less than two minutes long, but it felt like an eternity as I watched so many Black people being killed. I can't begin to tell you how hard it was to watch not only because of what happened to my mom, but also because of what happened to the other innocent people. None of them deserved to be targeted, hunted, and killed like animals and the sheer brutality of it angered me beyond measure.

Like others that were in the store, I wish my mother had been able to either flee or take cover. But speaking from personal experience, it is a deeply traumatic thing when someone draws a gun on you. The body is programmed to respond with a fight-or-flight response, but with her age and physical impairments, my mother was not going to escape. Even if she was able to run, she wouldn't have been able to outrun a bullet.

After seeing the video, as horrific as it was, a small part of me felt relieved. I had been beating myself up for not calling to check on my mom as soon as Rosh told me about the shooting at Tops when she picked me up from work. And the guilt I felt for not going to Tops immediately when my family told me that my mom was there was eating me alive because I thought there was something I could've done to prevent her death. But now, I realized that there was absolutely nothing I could've done. My mom was killed in less than two minutes from the time the killer arrived at Tops and started shooting people outside. By the time I left my shift at work, my mom was already dead.

I put my cell phone on the coffee table and glanced at the clock on the wall. It was a little after 10 a.m. and I was already drained emotionally, mentally, and physically. I wanted to climb back into the bed with Rosh to sleep it off but feared having another nightmare. So, as Porkchop played with her chew toy on the living room floor, I grabbed one of the picture albums and started flipping through pages containing pictures of me and my mom over the years, from pictures of me as a naked baby to pictures of me graduating from college. And while I glanced at the pictures, tears began to form again because I knew no new pictures would be added.

Suddenly, Rosh walked into the living room wearing her plushy robe and house slippers. "Hey baby," she said before giving me a kiss and sitting on the couch next to me. "How'd you sleep?"

"I slept okay. But Rosh, I watched the video. It was brutal. My mom and the others were hunted like animals and being shot in the head left and right."

"Oh no, baby!" Her eyes widened. "He didn't shoot your mom in the head, did he?"

I didn't say a word, I just started blinking rapidly trying to hold back the tears. She immediately held my hand as both of our eyes teared up.

"Watching my mom and the others die in the inhumane way they did lit a fire in me, Rosh." I said. "I can't keep sitting on the sidelines doing nothing. I need to get involved in the fight against racism and injustice. I need to man up and do something—I just don't know what."

Rosh smiled and I could tell she was proud of me. "I have faith in you. I know you'll figure it out."

Rosh gave me a kiss, grabbed the dog leash, and proceeded to take Porkchop outside. As I continued sitting on the couch, thinking about my future, I felt lost and wanted to call my mom for guidance, but there's was no point because I knew no one would answer the phone.

Chapter 11

U Don't Know – JAY Z

I was in a confused state of mind and just couldn't get the images of my mom and the other Black people I saw being killed out of my head. I still didn't know what I should do, why this happened, or what was next, and there were still so many other things I still didn't know— I mean, I knew that the killer was a White eighteen-year-old racist who livestreamed his killing spree on social media. I knew that he targeted the eastside of Buffalo because it has the highest concentration of Black people in the city and his goal was to kill as many Black people as possible. And I knew that he visited Tops previously to scope it out. But I didn't know if he was raised by white supremacists or if he was the only person in his family who was a racist. I didn't know how he got the semi-automatic weapon he used and how he was able to get it at the age of eighteen. And I didn't know so many other things. So, after calling my employer, thanking them for the donations they raised to help me, and resigning from my position, I grabbed my laptop from the kitchen counter and did an online search for the keywords 'Buffalo

Shooting Tops' to start filling in the gaps. Seconds later, my screen was flooded with search results that I sorted in chronological order by date.

In an article posted online by AP News, I found answers to some of my questions. The killer's name was Peyton Gendron and he arrived at Tops wearing bulletproof military gear. The reason the video felt like I was watching a first-person shooter videogame was because he was wearing a helmet camera, just like the reporter said on the phone. At that time, authorities were describing the mass shooting as a hate crime and "racially motivated violent extremism" and that three of the four Black people he shot outside before entering the store died. When I read this, I instantly knew from what I saw in the video that the two women he shot in the head and the man lying on his back behind the trunk were the ones who died.

As I continued reading the article, I discovered that the killer created a manifesto that detailed his "racist, anti-immigrant, and antisemitic beliefs", and that he purchased the rifle he used legally."[3]

But one of the most heartbreaking things I learned was that many of the victims who died that day were senior citizens between the ages of sixty-two and eighty-six.

Suddenly, Rosh came back into the apartment with Porkchop. "Baby, Trisha just called. She said the Bills are going to be at Tops today. Do you want to go?"

"Absolutely not. I'm not ready to deal with people yet and I'm definitely not ready to go to the location where I watched my mom get murder just a few days ago."

Later that night, I took Porkchop outside to use the bathroom and ran into the neighbor who lives down the hall. After offering me his condolences, he said that he went to Tops to see the Buffalo Bills and was surprised that the Buffalo Sabre's and the Buffalo Bandits were there, too. According to the neighbor, they served hot meals to the community and passed out much needed groceries because Tops was closed for business and there wasn't another large grocery store in east Buffalo.

On the morning of May 19th, my phone rang for the first time in days as Rosh sat in the living room watching news coverage of the killer's indictment by a grand jury.

"Hello?"

"Mark Talley?"

"Yes."

"Hello Mr. Talley, this is Ben Crump. How are you today, sir?"

Immediately, I was struck with shock. I had the nation's leading civil rights attorney on the phone, and I was at a loss for words.

"Hello Mr. Crump," I replied, trying to remain calm. "I'm good, hope you're doing well yourself. What can I help you with."

"Mark. I'm here in Buffalo. Can you meet me at Honnors Law Firm now? I want to discuss the terrible racist mass shooting at Tops with you."

"I'm on my way."

After getting the address to Honnors Law Firm, a prestigious local law firm, I hung up the phone and after giving Rosh a quick update and requesting an Uber, I was on my way. I was determined not to keep him waiting because there wasn't a single Black person in America who didn't know who Ben Crump was—I mean, to everyone in the Black community, he was the voice of the voiceless.

As I got closer to the law firm, a part of me still couldn't believe that I was less than twenty minutes away from meeting the man who represented the families of Trayvon Martin, George Floyd, Breonna Taylor, Ahmaud Arbery, Daunte Wright, and so many others. And I can't lie, I was excited.

When I arrived at Honnors Law Firm, the secretary greeted me and offered me some water, coffee, and a newspaper. Then, she walked me down the hallway to a big conference room where I was introduced to local attorney William Honnors, attorney Ben Crump, and Ben Crump's investigator.

Over the next hour, the investigator took notes while Ben, William, and I discussed the shooting at Tops and other unfortunate tragedies going on in the world. There was a funny moment when William and I thought we attended the same school—Canisius. Then, we realized that he was talking about Canisius College, and I was talking about Canisius High School.

Afterwards, Ben informed me that they were representing some of the other families whose loved ones were killed at Tops and were going to hold everyone who played a role in the tragedy accountable including the gun manufacturers, gun distributors, social media sites, and possibly even the killer's parents. And when they offered to represent me, I didn't need any time to think about it. I simply said, "Where do I sign?"

A few minutes later, we signed some contracts, and they officially became my attorneys that day.

I can't tell you how relieved I was to know that these powerful attorneys were going to fight with everything in their power to get my mom the justice she so richly deserved. In fact, I was so relieved to be represented by them that my brain really didn't process the other thing that I agreed to in the meeting with Ben and William until after I returned home.

"Rosh!" I screamed, pushing the front door open.

Porkchop immediately ran towards me and jumped on my leg. "I called Rosh, not you, Porkchop!" I said, gently pulling her down.

Rosh quickly turned the corner. "What's wrong?" She asked. "Didn't it go well?"

"It went great! But there's a press conference with Ben Crump and Reverend Al Sharpton at four-thirty today and I agreed to speak!"

"Wow, Reverend Al Sharpton? That's great, I'm so proud—"

My eyes became as big as donuts. "No Rosh! Not great!" I shook my head briskly. "Not great at all!"

When Ben Crump told me about the press conference and gave me an opportunity to speak, it sounded like a good way to get involved. I had been silent about my mom's death for far too long and wanted everyone to know what was taken from me. And I wanted to show them a picture of my mom so they could see who she was. But when I got home, I realized what I had agreed to and began to panic. I had no clue what I was going to say, trying to decide if I should write something down or just give my speech freestyle.

Rosh could tell that I was worked up and suggested that I lay down and think about what I was going to say, so I did. But as soon as my head hit the pillow, my mind was flooded with questions:

What if I forget the words I want to say about my mom?

What if I drop her picture while I'm speaking?

What if my loafers make me trip?

What if I open my mouth and nothing comes out?

What if something makes me laugh?

What if I need to use the bathroom in the middle of my speech?

What if I'm so nervous I accidentally fart?

As I continued lying in bed freaking myself out, I finally fell asleep.

At 3 p.m., Rosh woke me up. And after taking a quick shower and getting dressed, I put on a pair of black boots instead of the loafers I was planning to wear. I also grabbed the eight by ten size picture frame containing a beautiful picture of my mom and Malcolm off the dresser. This was going to be my first time doing any kind of public speaking, and I knew having my mom's picture would help—I need my mom and Rosh to be there with me.

Since I was still freaking out even after resting and knew this was going to be a stressful and intense day, I grabbed two THC gummies from the container in my nightstand and ate it. Edibles have been an invaluable source of help to me over the past few years. Not only did they help to control my seizures when I had epilepsy, but they also enabled me to manage my anxiety levels and feel more relaxed when they were at their peak. More importantly, they enabled me to manage my introverted nature and cope with social situations that involve large groups of people. And as I thought about speaking at my first press conference, I definitely needed to control my anxiety and introverted nature.

The THC gummies worked great and about thirty minutes later, Rosh and I were on our way to the press conference at Antioch Baptist Church. As we drove, I was definitely under the influence of the THC gummy because I was laughing at everything I saw outside and was having some interesting thoughts. "I don't think you should walk to close to me when we get to the church, Rosh" I said out of the blue.

"Why not?"

"You know how long it's been since I entered a church. What if I get struck by lightning? Do you really want to be walking right next to me?"

Rosh started laughing. "I'll take my chances."

When we arrived at the church, I immediately noticed numerous camera men and women setting up equipment directly in front of the church. It was at that moment that I was grateful for the instructions I received to enter the church through the door on the side of the building that was off the parking lot.

After parking the car, Rosh and I entered the church through the side door as instructed and were taken to a private room with about a dozen people whose loved ones were killed at Tops, along with my beautiful mom. Although everyone was cordial, the mood was somber as some people quietly wept and others seemed weary.

We sat down at a long rectangular table with the families of the other victims and a few minutes later, Ben Crump and Reverend Al Sharpton walked in. I'll be honest, the excitement that I felt when I received the call from Ben Crump was the same level of excitement that I had when I saw Reverend Al Sharpton. I'd even say that I was star struck because everybody and I do mean everybody in the Black community knows who Reverend Al Sharpton is. He's been a pillar in Black America for decades and has been at the forefront of the fight for civil rights.

After Reverend Sharpton met with us and prayed for our families, Mr. Crump briefed us on what to expect during the press conference and the order in which each person would speak. When I realized that I was going to be the first family member to speak after Reverend Sharpton, Mr. Crump, and Mr. Honnors, I was so glad the gummies still had me feeling chill.

When it was time for the press conference to begin, everyone in the private room exited the church through the same side door that we entered. I held up the picture of my mom and kept it up as we walked to the entrance of the church and gathered on the stairs in front of the reporters and camera men and women. Because I was the tallest person there, I stood towards the back of the stairs and continued holding up my mom's picture while Reverend Sharpton, Mr. Crump, and Mr. Honnors gave their powerful speeches. By the time they were finished, my arms were burning like they were on fire.

At this point, Mr. Crump invited me to the podium to speak. When I made my way to the front of the steps, I held my mom's picture in my hands and spent a few seconds showing it to the reporters. Then, I began my speech.

"The last time I spoke with my mother was on Mother's Day. I sent her a text message saying, 'Happy Mother's Day'. She replied back, 'thank you'. And that was the last time. That was it.

I never would've thought that would be the last time I would speak to her or hear her voice. I never would've thought my mother would be shot dead—have a bullet go through the right temple on her head because a White supremacist scouted, put a manifesto online, Twitched about it, wrote on 4Chan about it, came to Buffalo apparently a few days prior—found a community of low socio-economic status to plan his hate attack.

I constantly think about what could've been done. And it seems like—it's Groundhog's Day, like how many times have we seen a young White supremacist post on a far-right winged social media site what they plan on doing, what type of people they hate, who they want to target—they go out, buy a semi-automatic rifle. I mean myself, I can't even go to a local gun store to even just shoot a round without a conceal and carry permit but somehow an eighteen-year-old is easily able to just buy an illegally modified semi-automatic rifle and, like I said, it's just Groundhog's Day like we've seen this over and over and over again. Honestly speaking I wouldn't be surprised if another event happens like this down the line.

I never thought that this would happen in Buffalo. It's hard for me to imagine the city in which I grew up in, the neighborhood which I grew up in, the Tops on Jefferson which I went to plenty of times growing up, that would be the place of the next terrorist attack, the first terrorist attack I believe here in the United States. And it seems like people of color are becoming—they used to say we're second-class citizens. I believe we're third-class citizens now 'cause depending on what type of animal somebody has—you know, that dog is considered family and it seems like over the past century like it's known—people of low socio-economic status, people of color, this really is not our home.

You had it in 1920s in Tulsa when you saw African Americans start doing good for themselves, you had a bunch of White people, bunch of Klansmen, bunch of racists just destroy it. You had it throughout the sixties or seventies when veterans, Black veterans, were coming home after serving their country fighting in Vietnam. They couldn't even get a job here. You had it in the eighties with the crack epidemic when you had African Americans getting addicted to this—they didn't try to help them out. They didn't try to get them some substance abuse counseling. They were either killed or sent to prison compared to what's going on now with the opioid crisis, the first thing they try to do is get you on some type of addiction center, some rehab, some counseling. Last time I heard, I haven't even heard any opioid people getting Rico charges, but you have rappers getting Rico charges.

So, like I said, we're not even considered second class citizens no more, depending on what type of dog a family may have that dog is considered more family than a regular Black person you see walking down—so hopefully this is the last event. Honestly, I don't think it is and I don't think it will be for a long time.

Once again, the fact that an eighteen-year-old man can easily purchase a semi-automatic rifle and yet people check, people claim the gun laws are too strict or we're trying to tread on their right to buy guns. It's just sad and depressing and my mom showed to be a victim of this. Because somebody woke up, decided they didn't like Black people, and shot a hollow point bullet just right here with her fiancé watching hiding in the cooler as best as he could, and he ended up getting scratches all over his chest and arms. My mother's fiancé had to watch her die with a hollow point bullet going through her right temple."

Now, just to be clear, Malcolm didn't see my mom at the moment that she was shot while standing in the grocery aisle. He saw her afterwards.

After my speech ended, I went back to my original position on the stairs and other family members were given an opportunity to share their heartbreaking stories. And as I stood next to Rosh on the stairs and listened to their gut-wrenching stories about the loved ones they lost at Tops and the devastation to their lives that followed, I realized that my pain was their pain and it made me more determined than ever to turn our collective pain into a powerful purpose that would benefit our entire community, not just the families of the victims.

3. Thompson, Carolyn, Wawrow, John, Balsamo, Michael, and Collins, Dave. "10 dead in Buffalo supermarket attack police call hate crime". AP News, May 14, 2022. https://apnews.com/article/buffalo-supermarket-shooting-442c6d97a073f39f99d006dbba40f64b

CHAPTER 12
Who Gon Stop Me – JAY Z - Kanye West

The press conference was followed by an evening church service during which Reverend Sharpton and several other pastors preached. And as I sat and actively listened, I felt like I was on the verge of becoming more than I had been before May 14th and believed that my mom was proud of me for not only giving the first public speech I'd ever given, but also for attending a church service for the first time since I was twelve years old.

When Rosh and I made it back home, I decided to stop shielding myself from news coverage about May 14th and changed the location on my phone's news app back to Buffalo. My mom always said that knowledge is power and after watching the video and seeing the sheer brutality of white supremacy, I wanted to educate myself and do what I could to create an environment where Black people in east Buffalo could not only survive living while Black but also thrive.

On the morning of May 21st, I received a phone call from my family offering to handle the cremation, funeral, and repast arrangements for my mom and, I'll be honest, I was grateful. I couldn't handle seeing my mom with two holes in her head and with her face disfigured and was glad that her siblings were willing to step in. I was also so overwhelmed by everything that I had experienced and learned since May 14th and really didn't know the first thing about planning a funeral or repast.

I was also grateful to Reverend Al Sharpton and the National Action Network for offering to cover the costs of my mom's funeral.

Later that day, I began receiving phone calls from various members of my family telling me that Tops had created a GoFundMe called the *5/14 Survivors Fund* to raise money for the employees and families of the victims killed on May 14th. They also said that the Buffalo Bills were actively raising funds to donate to the *5/14 Survivors Fund* through the sale of 'Choose Love' shirts.

I wanted to know more information, so I called Tops and spoke with a customer service agent who confirmed the information I received about the *5/14 Survivors Fund*. She said that Tops made an initial donation of five hundred thousand dollars to kick the fundraiser off, but that over one million dollars in donations had been received so far.

I wasn't overly concerned about the fundraiser at this point. That is, until I received a call the next day while I was helping Rosh cook breakfast. The call was from a woman who introduced herself as someone whose cousin was murdered ten years ago during a mass shooting at a movie theater in Aurora, Colorado. When I heard this, I put the call on speaker so that Rosh could listen, too.

The woman said that immediately following the massacre in Aurora, Colorado, major non-profits and private citizens created GoFundMe's claiming to be raising money to help the families of the victims but knowing that they were not legally required to turn over any money raised if they didn't specifically state this in the description of the GoFundMe. She urged me to pay attention to the fundraisers claiming to be raising money to help the victims' families in the Buffalo shooting at Tops.

After thanking her for the heads up and hanging up, Rosh and I sat down to eat breakfast. "People are really sick," I said. "They would seriously scam the families of people killed out of money donated to help them?"

"That's horrible, but I believe it," Rosh replied, shaking her head. "I remember all the scammers that surfaced during Covid."

When Rosh brought up Covid, I knew that I wanted to do something to prevent scammers and schemers from trying to make a profit off the tragedy. And after meeting the other families of people killed at Tops at the press conference, I was determined not to let scammers, false witnesses, or anyone else profit from my mom's death or the deaths of the others. And I was not going to sit back and let money that was donated from people's hearts end up in the wrong hands.

After eating breakfast, Rosh left to run errands, and I grabbed my laptop and sat back down at the kitchen table. I was eager to search for the *Buffalo 5/14 Survivors Fund* to see how the description was written before I started reviewing the other fundraisers that claimed to be raising money for the families of the victims killed at Tops.

After booting my computer up, I did an online search and found the *Buffalo 5/14 Survivors Fund* on GoFundMe. The description stated the following:

> *On May 14, 2022, the Buffalo community suffered a devastating act of violence when a gunman opened fire at the Tops Friendly Market on Jefferson Avenue, killing ten people and wounding three. Many have asked how to help.*
>
> *In partnership with Tops, the National Compassion Fund has established the Buffalo 5/14 Survivors Fund to provide direct financial assistance to the survivors of the deceased and those directly affected by this tragedy.*
>
> *One hundred percent of the contributions donated to this fund will go directly to the victims and survivors of this atrocity. Qualifying charitable donations to this fund are tax deductible…*

The description clearly stated that one hundred percent of donations received would be given directly to survivors. So, as I reviewed the descriptions of other fundraisers that claimed to be raising money to help the families impacted by the tragedy at Tops, I made sure their intent was clearly stated in the description. I even went a step further and tried to contact the organizers of each fundraiser to make sure they were aware that I was the son of a victim killed at Tops and was aware of their fundraiser.

On May 24th, I began hearing rumors from various people that an organization called the National Compassion Fund was coming to Buffalo to take over the GoFundMe account that Tops created and to raise more money to give to the families impacted by the tragedy on May 14th. I'd never heard of the National Compassion Fund, but people were saying that a ton of money was being collected and yet no one from the National Compassion Fund had reached out to me or any of the other families. As you can imagine, I was confused—I mean, if all these funds are being collected on behalf of the victims' families, how come no one had contacted any of us?

And I had questions about who the National Compassion Fund considered a victim:

Was a victim somebody who died that day?

Was a victim somebody that got shot that day?

Was a victim somebody that almost got shot that day?

Was a victim somebody that saw the shooter and now has PTSD?

Was a victim someone that was on a property at Tops?

These were legitimate questions that I needed answers to and I'm sure the other family members wanted answers as well.

On May 27th, the funeral that my family arranged for my mom was held at Mt. Aaron Baptist Church and I wasn't told until the last minute that I was scheduled to give the eulogy. I didn't have any prepared remarks and had never given a eulogy, so initially, I did what I always do and used dark humor to cope. I remember saying something to the effect of: Giving this eulogy next to the Honorable Reverend Al Sharpton today, I can only hope lightning doesn't strike me as I'm standing next to this cross right now because it's been a long time.

After that, I just spoke from the heart. I talked about my mom and how she loved calling her sisters and other family members and inviting them to our house to watch Lifetime movies. I talked about how she enjoyed baking cookies for her family to enjoy while visiting her. I talked about how she was extroverted and sociable which was so different than me. And I made it a point to mention that there was no reason a person should have an AR-15 at home to protect their family.

I also appreciated the powerful words spoken by Reverend Sharpton and Mr. Crump about my mom, the other victims of the Tops racially motivated terrorist attack, the need for economic improvements on the eastside of Buffalo, and the need to address the mass shootings that continue to occur in America.

But I'll be honest, I wasn't happy with the funeral my family planned. It seemed amateurish. They had cousins singing and reading poetry who were too emotional to do it properly. I could have hired professionals for this. Instead of a private ceremony, they somehow made it open to the public, which was uncomfortable for me—I mean, I was running into my mom's exes and people claiming to be family who shouldn't have been there. This should have been a private event.

At the repast, family members were smoking right outside the door and although I'm in no position to judge, it was inappropriate for a funeral. I stayed at the repast for only five minutes before I left.

I don't blame my family for how bad the funeral was because I should've taken responsibility and organized it myself instead of putting the responsibility on someone else, which was not the right thing to do. And although my mom was cremated since we couldn't have an open casket, I couldn't understand the reason that over twenty small urns containing my mom's ashes were made. *Twenty!*

On May 28th, Reverend Sharpton invited me to attend another Tops victim's funeral and I had an opportunity to meet Vice President Kamala Harris before the funeral began. Meeting her was such an honor and I was glad to receive her recommendation for a book she encouraged me to read called *The Deepest Well*.

Over the next two weeks, I found myself growing increasingly concerned about the millions of dollars in donations that had been raised as part of the *5/14 Survivors Fund*, and I wasn't the only one who was concerned. Family members of the other Top victims were concerned, too, because weeks had passed, nearly three million dollars had been raised, and no one from the National Compassion Fund had contacted any of us. We felt like we were being kept in the dark.

On June 9th, the son of another victim who was killed at Tops and I took our grievances to the media and met with a reporter at ABC7. During the interview, I expressed my gratitude for the millions of dollars that were donated. "From the bottom, bottom, bottom of my heart I really want to thank every single person who donated," I said. "You saw a terrorist attack happen and that touched you to make you want to donate. And no words could express how appreciative I am."

But I also expressed my frustration because no one had contacted us to explain the process and the word on the street was that we weren't going to receive the money intended for us until December. Waiting until December to disburse the funds to the families meant that none of us would get the closure we needed to begin moving on for another six months.

"At the very first press conference I did with Benjamin Crump and Al Sharpton, I said this is Groundhog's Day related to these mass shootings," I said. "Now, having to constantly talk about my mother, the Compassion Fund, GoFundMe, donations—I'm now really living Groundhog's Day on an everyday basis."[4]

Our interview must have had an impact because the next day, the families of the Tops victims and the people who were shot at Tops met with the organizers of the National Compassion Fund about all the money that was coming in and the meeting went very well. The organizers were transparent and put our minds at ease as they told us who they are, what they do, what they're all about, and how they determine the process for distributing money to the families. They also informed us that a steering committee consisting of about twenty-three people in Buffalo who were in positions of authority had been formed and it was their job to decide how much money one person's life was worth. "That's a tough job," I said. "A job I definitely wouldn't want."

During the meeting, we spent a great deal of time talking and getting to know each other, and when they explained to us how they were going to break down the word 'victim', and told us the location in proximity to Tops that a person had to be in order to be classified as a victim, I was all ears. But what really caught my attention was the breakdown of payment categories that were established as follows:

Category A was the highest designated category. People in this group would receive the highest payout because they had a loved one who was killed.

Category B consisted of people who were shot or injured as a result of the shooter.

Category C consisted of people who were inside Tops at the time of the shootings and were able to escape uninjured.

Category D consisted of people and employees who were at Tops that day.

Category E consisted of employees of Tops who weren't there that day.

Initially, I thought there were too many categories and felt that the word 'victim' should be defined as someone whose loved one was killed at Tops on May 14th, or someone who was shot by the racist shooter and survived. My thoughts changed, however, after I had a conversation with the executive director of the National Compassion Fund.

The executive director said that there were plenty of other national tragedies that had occurred in the U.S. and although there were physical victims, there were a lot of mental victims. He then told me a story about how one woman got paid by the National Compassion Fund from the donations collected off the estate of her loved one and that there was a man who was at that location as well during the tragedy. This man, who had no relationship with the woman, held her loved one until she died so she wouldn't be afraid.

But, one day, the man showed up on her doorstep crying because he was traumatized from the experience of holding her loved one and watching her die. Through his story, I was able to see that there were people who may not have lost loved ones, but who developed PTSD from these tragedies. In the end, I realized that everybody who was at Tops that day could've been affected even if they didn't look hurt.

During the meeting, I also discovered that all the work I did in reviewing the fundraisers that claimed to be raising money for the families of the Tops victims was not necessary because they have attorneys who review all fundraisers and ensure that proceeds are sent to the National Compassion Fund for distribution.

On June 27th, I began the process of becoming the administrator and head of my mother's estate because I felt it was my responsibility as her only son. And because of the different things that I had gotten involved with over the last several weeks, I was keeping myself busy and thought that I had moved past the point of being angry, but I was wrong.

---

4.   Schwartz, Michael. "Sons of two women killed in Tops shooting look for answers about Buffalo 5/14 Survivors Fund distribution." 7ABC Buffalo WKBW, June 9, 2022. https://www.wkbw.com/news/local-news/buffalo-mass-shooting/sons-of-two-women-killed-in-tops-shooting-look-for-answers-about-buffalo-5-14-survivors-fund-distribution?_amp=true

CHAPTER 13

Halfcrazy – Musiq Soulchild

Over the summer, the families of the victims of Tops continued to meet with the National Compassion Fund's organizers and, as I suspected, people started trying to scam. Some people snuck into meetings claiming to be a victim eligible for payment because they either:

1) drove to Tops after the shootings occurred, stayed and watched, and now can't work anymore due to PTSD.

2) lived down the street from Tops and no longer felt safe, developed PTSD, and couldn't work anymore.

3) were on their way to Tops and believe they're a victim because if they made it to the store in time, they could've been shot.

4) was scheduled to work at Tops but don't want to work there anymore out of fear.

In my opinion, if you were in the Tops store or parking lot, or even if you were working there on that fateful day, you were a victim of this tragedy. However, I cannot fathom why some people tried to fight or scam their way into becoming a victim when they were blessed with the greatest gift of all: their lives. They were fortunate enough to walk away unscathed, with no physical or emotional wounds and, sadly, the same cannot be said about the families and friends of the ten people who lost their lives on May 14th, or the three people who were injured.

Some of the most heartbreaking incidents that took place occurred when people tried to sneak into the National Compassion Fund meetings that were dedicated to the families claiming that they had suffered some kind of mental trauma as a result of driving to Tops after everything had happened and witnessing the chaotic environment.

Adding insult to injury, was a man that I had never met in my entire life and didn't even know existed, let's call him Lying Ryan, who began speaking to the media claiming that he and my mother were best friends who baked cookies together and that she was his caretaker. He even had the nerve to say that he was going to publish a book with their favorite recipes and donate the proceeds to the victims' families. Of course, there was no truth to any of this, as my mother had no relationship with this man whatsoever.

To make matters worse, the National Compassion Fund contacted me to inform me that there had been several attempts to file a claim on behalf of my mother from both related and unrelated people. When I discovered that all of this was going on, I was glad that I took the necessary steps to become the administrator of my mother's estate. And when everything was approved and I became one hundred percent in charge of any allocated distributions for my mom's estate, I breathed a sigh of relief.

Over the summer when approximately four million dollars in donations had been received, people began criticizing the National Compassion Fund for various reasons. Some people were frustrated because they wanted to receive their money right away; some people were questioning the reason for the delay in releasing funds to the victims; some accused the National Compassion Fund of holding the money unnecessarily; and some people were a little more assertive saying, "the donated money is ours and we wanted it now".

Although I understood the frustration that was being expressed by various people, after we had our initial meeting with the National Compassion Fund and they provided us with complete transparency, I knew that they had our best interest at heart. And when they informed us that they wanted to keep the fundraiser open as long as possible to give everyone who wanted to donate a chance to do so, I trusted that they knew what they were doing.

On October 24th, the National Compassion Fund informed us that when the fundraiser was closed to donations on September 20th, and that an additional three million dollars in donations had been received making the total amount to be distributed to the victims over seven million dollars. They informed us that donations had been received from all around the world and if they had given in to the pressure and closed the fundraiser in July or August, we would've missed out on receiving an additional three million dollars.

In the end, the donations were distributed to approximately 160 people who were classified as victims, but the majority of funding was distributed to the ten families whose loved ones were killed at Tops, and the three people who were shot by the killer and survived.

Again, I am so grateful to each and every person who donated to help me and the other victims of the racially motivated mass shooting at Tops. My life was changed in the worst possible way on May 14th and although I have not fully recovered as of yet and I miss my mom more than words can ever say, your love and support has given me hope that I will one day find myself looking forward and not backwards and on the path to healing.

And I'm very, very grateful to the National Compassion Fund for everything they did to help me and the other victims. Although our relationship started off rocky, I'm proud to say that I definitely have a great relationship with them now and will always be grateful for the love and support they extended to all of the families impacted by the Tops tragedy.

Now, I look forward to turning my pain into a powerful purpose that will benefit the eastside of Buffalo, honor my mom in the best way possible, and help our community heal from the tragedy that happened the day the devil came to Buffalo.

CHAPTER **14**

Life of The Party – Kanye West featuring Andre 3000

If you haven't heard the song, *Life of the Party* by Kanye West featuring Andre 3000, I strongly encourage you to listen to it before continuing to read this. I first heard this song a few months ago, and it perfectly captures how I feel and how my life has been since my mother passed away.

I wish she could just say something to me, in any way, shape, or form. I feel so lost without her. This feeling happens more and more frequently, and it's gotten to the point where I find myself staring at her pictures and crying uncontrollably. Losing my mother has left me feeling confused, lost, and sad, often without warning.

Now, I don't want to paint a picture that makes it appear that me and my mom were glued at the hip because we weren't. But we did have our own special connection. And the pain of losing her has been immense and has been made worse by the fact that it was an act of hatred and racism that took her away from this world—away from me. I know I'm not alone in feeling this way—the attack has affected so many lives, including the lives of those who are close to me and those who aren't.

Even songs on the radio or my playlist that I know were her favorites make me break down. I can't even listen to *Been Around the World* by Puffy anymore because it was one of her favorites. Because of this, I'm becoming more detached from society and colder, and it's having a negative impact on my relationship with my wife, Rosh.

I wish I could be the man I was before my mom's death, but I fear I'll never be that person again. Even as I'm writing this, tears are streaming down my face, and my dog Porkchop is trying to lick them away. It's almost as if my mother's spirit is in her, trying to tell me it's okay. I doubt it, but it brings me a sense of comfort. Plus, I hope her spirit isn't in Porkchop because she licks all over herself and I don't want her ass particles on my mom's mouth.

I also find myself filled with a mixture of jealousy and envy for the families of the other victims that day who lost their mothers because they got to spend more time with their mothers than I did. It hurts so much because I had the opportunity to make more memories with my mom but chose not to take advantage of it. Now, I crave every moment I could have shared with my mother and wish I could pick up the phone and call her. Like I said at the beginning of this book, I still send messages to her phone or on Facebook, but the silence that follows is deafening.

The loss of my mother is even more painful because it was due to gun violence and systemic racism. It's a pain that never goes away, no matter how much time passes. My mother was taken from me by an eighteen-year-old racist who illegally modified an assault rifle and used it to kill innocent people. It is something that I can't seem to wrap my head around still. This tragedy was one hundred percent the result of a system that perpetuates racism and violence, and it's something that can no longer be ignored.

I know that it's impossible to understand the pain that I feel, but for all of you reading this, I want you to understand the consequences of these reckless acts. My mother was an amazing person who didn't deserve to be taken away like that. And the pain of her loss grows more and more each day, and it will never go away.

I'm here to tell you that no one deserves to experience this kind of tragedy, and that we must do something to end this cycle of violence. We can't allow these weapons to be used in such a way, and we must take concrete steps to make sure that this never happens again. America is suffering from a malady that manifests itself in racism, homophobia, xenophobia, an unhealthy fixation on guns, a refusal to acknowledge the most dangerous being in the world is a young adult White male, and most significantly, socio-economic inequality. Sadly, America appears to be either too scared or too unwilling to seek medical attention for its affliction.

To conclude in a more optimistic light, something positive did come out of this unfortunate tragedy, and even saying the word 'positive' for me seems like too much. To cope with the loss of my mother, I began to volunteer my time at organizations on Jefferson Avenue helping out the residents in the community. Organizations such as World Central Kitchen, The Buffalo Urban League, Pastor James E. Giles and Back to Basic Ministries, and Leonard Lane and Buffalo F.A.T.H.E.R.S. This eventually led me to create my own nonprofit organization, Agents for Advocacy.

Agents for Advocacy seeks to spread awareness regarding systemic racism and socioeconomic inequality, with the hope of bringing about a world where one's race and environment do not determine their future. I'm determined to find a way to honor my mother's memory and to use her example to fight against racism and hatred. I believe that together we can create a better world, one in which such senseless acts of violence are no longer a part of our lives.

Since May 14th, we have organized and taken part in numerous socioeconomic events and classes in the east side of Buffalo. I have even been invited to serve as a paid public speaker, discussing the same matters I used to volunteer for. It is still amazing to me that I am getting paid to talk about things which I do for free. Had anyone told me that this would be the outcome of my loss, I would have punched them, as I was in no shape to talk to anyone. But I can tell you this, without a shadow of a doubt, I would trade it all just to hear my mother yell at me, hug me, joke with me, anything. If I could hear her again, I would trade it all. I wish my mom could be here to witness everything I've done and achieved. The sheer joy that would be on her face if she saw me buying my first house—I can only imagine! She would be so proud of the work I'm doing in the community. Although she may not be a fan of my style— I'm more of a tank top and sweatpants kind of person, while she preferred khakis and button-ups—I'm sure she would be proud of me regardless.

I know it comes from a place of love and kindness when people tell me that she is with me in spirit, but to be honest I don't want to hear that. I already know that spiritually she is with me; you could even argue that she is with me physically because her ashes are in my keychain that I take everywhere, and her birthdate is tattooed on my arm. But I want more than that. I want to be able to touch her and feel her presence, and I want her to be right by my side, to see all that I'm doing and achieving.

As a result of my work in the community, I have been labelled a public figure and a community leader, meaning I must conduct myself in a more appropriate manner. Some days it is difficult to stay calm, but I understand the importance of my rising status and the necessity of not being hot-tempered if I am to make meaningful change at a macro level. And although some days are more challenging than others, I am doing my best.

Through my organization, I strive to become the largest socioeconomic justice organization in the city, if not the state, so I can fight for what is right by any means necessary. As this book comes to an end, I urge all of you to become an agent for change in your family, your community, your job, and your city. By doing so, you, too, can become an AGENT FOR ADVOCACY.

Reflections

So, it's May 12th. After seven long months of hard work, my book is finally done. It was ready for pre-order on Amazon for Kindle, but unfortunately, it was taken off due to a glitch, but it's alright; these things happen in life. It was a great feeling to know that while my book was listed on Amazon, it was ranked as a number one best seller for new releases.

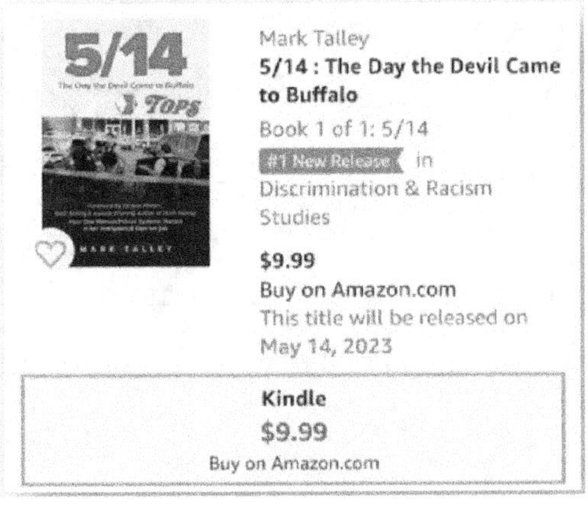

This upcoming weekend will mark the one-year anniversary of my mother's death and ironically Mother's Day. People have asked me how I feel about it, but I really don't know. I don't feel sad, nor do I feel any sorrow or pain. I feel nothing, yet maybe I just don't know how to feel.

Before I finish, I'd like to take a moment to thank everyone who has been by my side, especially Reverend Al Sharpton and the National Action Network for everything they did to assist me during my darkest hours including paying for my mother's funeral, and for sponsoring this book to help me shine a much-needed light on systemic racism, gun violence, and socioeconomic inequality.

I also want to dedicate this book to Tyler Lewis. The tragic death of Tyler Lewis at the University of Buffalo's Amherst campus is a stark reminder of the systemic racism and unequal justice system present in our country.

After the grand jury declined to press charges against the individual responsible for his death, Erie County D.A. John Flynn declared the stabbing justifiable. This decision left the family of Tyler Lewis with the same feeling of helplessness faced by many Black Americans in similar situations: the belief that if a White person kills a Black person, they can get away with it. The death of Tyler Lewis is just one of many examples of the unequal application of justice in our society and the impunity of White perpetrators. We must demand an end to this unjust system and strive for true justice and equality for all.

Me carrying my mom's ashes after her funeral

Long Live the Jefferson 10 Memorial
Artists: John Fredrick Daniels and Grady Lewis

Me hugging Reverend Al Sharpton during my mom's funeral

www.ingramcontent.com/pod-product-compliance
Lightning Source LLC
Chambersburg PA
CBHW051745250726
48659CB00001B/246